Studies in Society

A Gender Agenda

A sociological study of teachers, parents and pupils in their primary schools

Terry D. Evans

Sydney
ALLEN & UNWIN
Wellington London Boston

First published in 1988
Allen & Unwin Australia Pty Ltd
An Unwin Hyman company
8 Napier Street, North Sydney, NSW 2060 Australia

Allen & Unwin New Zealand Limited
60 Cambridge Terrace, Wellington, New Zealand

Unwin Hyman Limited
15–17 Broadwick St, London W1V 1FP, England

Allen & Unwin Inc.
8 Winchester Place, Winchester, Mass 01890 USA

National Library of Australia
Cataloguing-in-Publication entry:

Evans, Terry D. (Terry Denis).
A gender agenda: a sociological study of teachers, parents and pupils in their primary schools.

Bibliography.
Includes index.
ISBN 0 04 303009 2.

1. Sex discrimination in education. 2. Sex discrimination in education — Victoria — La Trobe River Valley — Case studies. 3. Educational sociology. 4. Sex differences in education. 5. Social structure. 6 Education, Elementary. I. Title. (Series: Studies in society (Sydney, N.S.W.)).

370.19

Set in 10/11pt Times by Setrite Typesetters, Hong Kong
Printed in Hong Kong by Dah Hua Printing Ltd

Preface

The research project which underpins this book was designed to demonstrate the links between the social structural features of society, especially gender, and the social processes which surround and comprise schools. The book is written with a range of readers in mind: academics, students, teachers and other people with an interest in educational, social and gender issues. It aims to provide an understanding of the ways in which gender affects the people whose lives are concerned principally with schooling: children, parents, teachers, administrators. In effect this book has something to say about all of us because, one way or another, we all go to school. The main focus is on the structures and processes of two primary schools and, although I have tried not to encumber the reader with volumes of theory, there is a gentle theoretical undercurrent throughout the book. Occasionally this undercurrent surfaces, especially in the first couple of chapters, into a stronger flow of discussion about contemporary social theory and research into gender.

However, those with a passion for immersing themselves in the details of school life can take some stepping stones through the first two chapters and then dive into Chapter 3. Throughout the book I have provided some small italicised sections written in a narrative style. It is hoped that the immediacy of these personal reflections will serve to counterpoint the necessarily more conventional style of the rest of the book.

To ensure confidentiality, names of people and places have been changed and other details altered. The first two chapters present the literature, theory and research methodology which informed the study. People who are less concerned about such matters can read the italicised sections as their stepping stones to Chapter 3 where the discussion about the schools and their communities commences. Other readers, perhaps students, may prefer to read the first two chapters and then return to re-read them after completing the book. Otherwise, start at the beginning and proceed to the end or, indeed, do your own thing!

A brief outline of our research is useful at this point. The project was entitled 'Gender Processes and Structures in the Primary School'. I am grateful for research funds provided by the Commonwealth Schools Commission under its Projects of National Significance scheme, however, I should emphasise that the views in this book do not necessarily represent those of the Commission. The research assistant, Rosemary Langmore and I carried out the work between September 1983 and February 1985. Two primary schools were selected: Tordale, which is a four teacher rural school with about 75 pupils; and Linfield, which is a town school with approximately 450 pupils and 25 teachers.

The principal foci of our research were the ways in which the social structural division of gender was evident in the schools and the ways in which it was negotiated and reconstructed by the people involved. In essence, we were recording matters of generation and gender, because we were as concerned to study the adults employed in or connected with the school as we were to study the children. Hence, it was as important to study gender division in a wrangle at a school council or union meeting, as it was to observe and record interactions between males and females in a school classroom. Therefore, this book divides its attention between the adult and child worlds of schooling.

Part I of the book deals with the adults' world of schooling. It shows how gender relationships affect adult lives and how adults bring these relationships to bear in their involvement with schools. Part II presents the children's world of schooling, not as an autonomous entity, but as one which has various interconnections with the adults' world. In particular, it focuses on the school curriculum and classroom life to explain the practice and reconstruction of gender divisions in schooling. The notion of a *gender agenda* is used to link the existing gender divisions in the adult world with those set for the children to understand, interpret and negotiate in their emerging social worlds. In accordance with common practice, I use 'agenda' (rather than 'agendum') as the singular form and, therefore, 'agendas' becomes the plural—my apologies to the purists.

I can proceed no further without acknowledging the contributions of others. The schools and their communities cooperated willingly and helpfully. The Education Department gave its permission to the project. Rosemary Langmore not only worked on the research

Contents

For Lesley and Gael

project, but also offered invaluable comments on the manuscript. Shirley Sampson encouraged me to do the research and has provided advice, comments and assistance throughout. Ron Wild gave kind and constructive criticisms of the manuscript during its production. Daryl Nation helped me sustain my energy during the research and writing, and he reviewed the chapters as they appeared. I shall not forget how these people—in different ways, to different degrees and in different circumstances—extended their friendship and generosity to me. I am especially indebted to Lesley Evans for her contribution to my understanding of gender, for her support during the research and her critical comments on the manuscript. Finally, I would like to acknowledge my appreciation of the constructive suggestions and editorial wisdom of Michelle Wright, an editor for Allen and Unwin.

She Stroke He
(Notes towards a unixex sub-language)

I like you
is uncertain of sex
and you can be plural too,
while us and them
is an old strategem
for dividing the world in two;
but he stroke she
and she stroke he
are a far more inviting sign
of sexual solidarity:
conjugations you can't decline

NEIL COURTNEY

1 Introduction

There was no doubt about it: Jenny could run. Even for a seven year old, she ran with a graceful efficiency that made the rest of the class look like knobbly-kneed pups chasing their tails. Other children could also run well, but their speed was born of effort and exertion; Jenny's speed came from the smooth, long stride of a good middle-distance runner.

It was a mild summer morning at Tordale primary school and Carmel Walls was taking her class of preps, ones and twos for a physical exercise session in the school grounds. Even though the school was small, with 76 children in three classes, its grounds were spacious, with plenty of grass and trees for the children to enjoy. Several parents, teachers and members of the rural community of Tordale had worked together over the years to build sports, recreation and play facilities in the school grounds. They had built an exercise track which wound its way through the tree-lined perimeter of the school grounds. Along its path there were beams to balance along, timber frames to climb, obstacles to leap and other physical challenges for the children. It was around the exercise track that Carmel Walls had sent her class for 'Huff n' Puff' time.

Jenny may have been the best runner, but by the time she had negotiated the balancing beam, three boys had caught up with her. They achieved this by running along the beam until they lost balance, then jumping off to run alongside. Jenny was amongst the leading group of about one third of the class as they clambered over the climbing frame. These children were competing quite seriously.

At the rear came Chantrelle and Lucinda; they were walking and talking their way around the exercise track, circling obstacles and apparently unconcerned about the race ahead of them. Bruce was a little ahead of them, dawdling and equally dismissive of the challenge set by his teacher. He lolloped over some barriers and avoided others. Carmel Walls gently ran the course, helping children across the obstacles, and dispensing praise, encouragement or admonishment as she saw fit. Her view of the race was from the middle: the leaders just in sight, the losers out of sight, and the middle group sharply in focus.

Jenny finished in fourth place and began playing a game with some other girls when they finished the course. The first boys to finish began to play their own game. A number of the children milled around Carmel Walls, overwhelming her with questions, requests to go to the drinking fountain and various titbits of information from their immediate concerns. Soon the attention shifted towards the stragglers who were aimlessly and lethargically completing the last part of the course. The class yelled at Bruce, Chantrelle and Lucinda to hurry up because they wanted to start playing the next game.

These three children were made for a different style of life than that symbolised by an exercise track. Chantrelle and Lucinda were two of a kind: small and slight, wearing cotton frocks and black patent leather shoes, their hair in pig-tails. Bruce, on the other hand, was short and obese, his body ballooning from school shorts, shirt and pullover. These three children seemed outsiders in a world of casual shorts, jeans and tracksuits.

This narrative describes an event which occurred during our field-work at Tordale primary school. It captured my thoughts because it says something about the *gender agenda* which we each race through every day. Let us look at the race on that February morning in 1984 in a way that provides links with social life in general.

Perhaps the whole event is a metaphor for the many challenging and competitive circumstances we face during our lives. Jenny was demonstrably the best athlete in the race, but this was not enough for her to win against boys who adhered less assiduously to the spirit and letter of the rules. Carmel Walls did not notice the boys' transgressions because of her position in the race. She stayed in the middle, although not as a racer. Her perceptions of the children and their performances influenced her actions. She knew the leading children were performing well because they were ahead of her, therefore, her efforts were better spent on those who were obviously in need and who, by virtue of their middle positions, were competitive. Chantrelle, Lucinda and Bruce became problems, for the class as well as Carmel Walls, when they were so far behind that everyone was delayed.

How can we explain and understand Jenny and Bruce? Or any of the other children? Or Carmel Walls? Or the gamut of circumstances which led to the observation of the race around the Tordale primary school exercise track? If these people and circumstances conform to a metaphor for life in general, how does this research project itself fit into the surrounding world?

Many authors have identified and explained elements of contemporary social life through their analyses of gender and education (see, Coats, 1983; Evans, 1983; Moskowitz, 1983 and Yates, 1987). Girls and women have been the subjects of most of this research, as part of a broader international cultural shift centred upon 'new wave feminism'. The present study is a product of these times, although tempered by some other debates in contemporary social theory and, of course, by the author's predilections and circumstances.

In essence, the research project set out to study the ways in which gender affected the life of primary schools. It was about the broader life of the schools, from their interaction with the various legal and administrative frameworks of the state and with their local communities, through to the interaction among the people who make up schools: pupils, parents and staff. The aim was to explain and understand pupils such as Bruce and Jenny, or teachers such as Carmel Walls, as individuals with biographies whose thin roots extend deep into the social structure. Similarly, the schools were studied as sites where these people coalesce to help construct the next generation of adults. In this sense the schools were studied as agencies, located within the social structure, whose purpose is to sustain and maintain it. It is worth considering some of the broader relationships between gender and education at this point.

Sex, gender and society

The words 'sex' and 'gender' are often used synonymously. In fact, both these words and their derivatives are good examples of how language and meaning change to reflect and facilitate cultural shifts. In this book the word *sex* refers to the biological attributes of female and male, and the word *gender* refers to the social and cultural features of femininity and masculinity. Since the resurgence of feminism over the past twenty years there has been some considerable debate about the origins of femininity, masculinity and more particularly, patriarchy—the domination of men and the subordination and oppression of women. Some people, typically conservatives and men, have sought to explain these social and cultural features by reducing them to simple biological differences between males and females. Hence, the terms 'biological reductionism' or 'biological determinism' are used to refer to the theory of how matters of gender can be reduced to, or seen to be determined by, biological differences (Dunlop, 1982).

Feminist writing challenges, both explicitly and implicitly, biological reductionism and determinism as explanations for gender differences in society. Gender is seen as socially constructed, that is, formed through the social processes through which all aspects of social life are made and given meaning within our culture (Berger and Luckmann, 1967). Hence, femininity and masculinity are seen to mean partly different things in different societies because of variations in the social structures and in the ways people have constructed their meanings of these terms.

A common finding in past and present societies is that men dominate women. Rubin (1975) argues an anthropological case, that the oppression of women in different societies is related to sexuality and human reproduction. Engels dates a significant change in gender relationships, from matrilineal to patrilineal, to the time when men began to claim the acquisition of property as part of their subsistence production, which they then passed on to their sons (Engels, 1968). He argues that the reproduction of sons became crucial and so subsistence production and human reproduction became inextricably linked to the development and maintenance of social institutions, especially the family. In contemporary feminist writing there has been some important debate about the ways in which people's relationships to the means of production and to human reproduction can be understood and explained. In essence, theories about one major social division, class, are being brought together with emerging theories about gender, in order to illuminate the explanation of both.

The family has been a focus of scrutiny in the pursuit of theory about class and gender relations because it is the basic unit of production and reproduction, as well as consumption, in society (David, 1982). It is clear that the term 'family' needs to be used in the widest sense to include the various forms of cohabitation in which people choose to live, love or reproduce. The family is usually the start of human reproduction and also of social reproduction, that is, reproducing the social and cultural features of society. In this way masculinity and femininity are reproduced, initially, through socialisation in the family. Mitchell (1974) uses psychoanalytic theory to explain the construction of masculinity and femininity in bisexual children according to their sex. She sees the symbolic power of the father in the unconscious as the root of the ideological control of patriarchy. This implies that the culture is shaped by a collective unconscious deference to the father, which translates itself, through a generalised subservience to masculinity, into patriarchy.

Although the family may well be a location for the type of psychological processes which Mitchell discusses it is also most clearly a location for the intersection of the social relations of production and reproduction. That is, the social relations concerned with productive labour, breadwinning, wage earning etc., and the social relations of reproductive labour, sexuality, child bearing, parenting etc. These social relations are complexly and inseparably intertwined within the family. For example, the organisation of domestic labour is not only concerned with children, but also with maintaining the productive capabilities of its adult members. Likewise, the wages of males have been set, at least partly, on the assumption that they will be supporting a family. Beechey (1979) explains the importance of not separating the production and reproduction relationships in developing theory about patriarchy. Rather, she argues for an analysis of the historical development of these interrelationships within the family as capitalist forms of patriarchy have burgeoned. Matthews (1984) shifts the debate in Australia about patriarchy towards a conceptualisation of gender order. This allows for matriarchal, patriarchal and egalitarian structures to be theorised together as forms of gender order.

When people form families the social relations of reproduction represent a significant symbolic and practical challenge which is founded in the gender order. The social relations involved begin to entangle women in a web of domestic labour, financial subservience, childbirth and parenting which few avoid or escape from. Even those who diminish or break the financial subservience find that much of the remaining web remains intact. Some feminists strive to produce 'a realisation that women and girls can work together, that they can overcome the obstacles which society puts in their way' (McRobbie and McCabe, 1981:5). In effect, a new gender order is being sought.

However, another web entangles men; it requires them to protect and materially support 'their' women and children, but it excludes them from most parenting and domestic labour. This latter web is rarely discussed in the literature, but its demands and exclusions are felt only too keenly by those men who have no paid work, who have to assume parenting alone or who take an equal responsibility for parenting. In a society with an egalitarian gender order, women and men could live and reproduce in settings, such as families, with as little difference in the organisation and sharing of domestic, parenting and breadwinning labour as the biology of human reproduction allowed. People who organise their lives this way find that many institutions and individuals resist or obstruct their efforts. In this sense both women and men are bound equally and differently by the traditional gender structures of society; although for most men the traditional circumstances suit them nicely.

Education and the reproduction of gender

One feature of the growth of modern societies has been the institutionalisation of agents of socialisation other than the family. Education and the mass media are now powerful agents of socialisation. They account for substantial amounts of labour and capital and they occupy a significant proportion of people's lives. Again, it is difficult to isolate the ways in which they, and the family, reflect and reproduce gender division in society. In discussing education or the mass media, it is possible to think of them as being part of a social or cultural process whereby masculinity, femininity and the other attributes of culture are reproduced.

Two of the most influential reproduction theorists, Althusser and Bourdieu, concur in seeing education as the most important arm of the state in reproducing both the forces of production and the relations of production. In this sense, education is seen as reproducing not only the technical and intellectual skills required to maintain production but also the beliefs and values necessary to maintain the social structure fitting the particular form of production which obtains. Althusser (1971) sees education as an 'ideological state apparatus' which inculcates the necessary means and beliefs into the rising generation in order to continue to reproduce the existing social order. In essence, the children of the working and ruling classes are equipped, through their different educational experiences, to believe in the appropriateness of their class positions, and to behave accordingly. Bourdieu and Passeron (1977) develop a theory along broadly similar lines to Althusser's, but which adopts certain concepts to explain the process through which ideological control is reproduced. For them the symbolic aspects of culture are crucial in this process: as 'cultural capital' which is passed on to the rising generations of the ruling class and as 'symbolic violence' which is perpetrated against the working class. Bourdieu (1977) argues that children are not destined to inherit a predetermined set of social relationships. Rather, in his view, they acquire values and beliefs—termed 'habitus'—which shape their future adult lives in relation to the class position of their families.

More recently, scholars are challenging some of the assumptions of reproduction theory whilst also recognising its contribution to the development of social theory (e.g. Apple, 1982a; 1982b; Giroux, 1983). Connell is one such person. He concludes that 'the reproduction of social relations is a chimera' which cannot logically occur, and that 'we cannot treat social structure as something...which occurs behind the backs of mortal people, who are inserted into their places by...a cosmic cannery called Reproduction' (1983:149). He argues that an 'intelligible succession' of practice is produced in contexts which historically have structural similarities. Each context has its own unique production of practice and 'it is the relation of practice between them' which is relevant 'not a relation of similarity between the structure today and the structure yesterday (but rather) the way one was produced out of the other' (1983:149). Giroux adopts a similar position in relation to reproduction and resistance theories of education and argues for 'a new radical pedagogy... drawn from a theoretically sophisticated understanding of how power, resistance, and human agency can become central elements in the struggle for critical thinking and learning' (1983:293). Both of these theorists, although perhaps more particularly Connell, consciously include gender as a social structural entity in their push for theoretical development. In terms of gender, masculinity and femininity are not simply reproduced from one generation to the next through education, mass media etc., but new forms of masculine and feminine practice are created sequentially through time. An *agenda* is formed of ideas, issues and problems flowing from previous practice which shapes engagement with the immediate practice. Gender is one element of the continuous formation and reformation of the *agenda*.

Connell researched and developed his theoretical position, with Ashenden, Kessler and Dowsett, in a study of schools, families and social division (class and gender) in Sydney and Adelaide (1982). Their aim was to move beyond a reproduction approach by immersing themselves in the study of people's explanations of their practice. They concentrated on working class and ruling class families and interviewed them about their social position, schooling, gender relations etc. By researching, rather than theorising about, the practice of people who occupied particular class and gender positions, Connell, Ashenden, Kessler and Dowsett intended to understand more clearly the nature and process of the production and practice of class and gender relations. Their findings reveal a complexity of beliefs, ideas and practices, and a capacity, especially through families, for creating and influencing the conditions of personal life which reproduction theory tends to deny.

In two research projects, Nation and I collected some similar findings (Evans and Nation, 1984). Amongst other things, we found that parents used their practical experience of the local labour market and their understanding of general labour market characteristics to guide, influence and, occasionally, create the conditions of work for their children. We found that such actions were also affected by the parents' developing interpretations of adult gender relationships, especially as they perceived such relationships affecting the adult lives of their children. Our evidence indicated that these families were not so much *reproducing* as *constructing* the conditions of their children's existences out of the material and intellectual resources at their disposal. Intellectual resources in this sense refers not only to the 'cultural capital' that Bourdieu and others describe, but also to the capacity for rational and creative thought about problems and their solutions. Such material and intellectual resources are affected by the practical conditions of each family in relation to its place within the social structure. We argued that some useful 'signposts towards theoretical and methodological progress' exist in recent Australian work including that of Connell, Ashenden, Kessler and Dowsett discussed above and also Baldock and Cass (1983), Burns, Bottomley and Jools (1983), Edgar (1980:180–205) and Williams (1981). Gaskell's (1983) research into Canadian adolescents' plans for family life also provides useful comparative evidence and analysis.

Gender division in the education system

It is often the case in educational research that the principal objects of study are the children. In some senses we may see this as most pertinent; after all is not schooling centrally concerned with children? The answer is that schooling is only for children to the extent that it conforms to adult interests. It may be argued that schools are very much adult institutions. They are run by adults (teachers etc.) for adults (parents, bureaucrats, politicians, or, more collectively, the state). The money which is expended on schooling largely goes on salaries to adults or on payments for the goods, services and buildings from which other adults derive their income or profits. The power to determine the general operation of schools rests with the state, and the power to determine the local operation of the school rests with, in Victoria as in most other States, school councils, principals, teachers and, in some cases, with non-governmental religious or secular organisations. Generally, the entire *agenda* of a school's life is set by adults, although this does not mean the pupils or students are merely passive recipients. Indeed, there is considerable evidence of the strategies students use to resist, make sense of or adjust to their compulsory school lives (e.g. Davies, 1984; Hargreaves, Hester and Mellor, 1975; Willis, 1977; Woods, 1980).

The research and writing about sex, gender and schooling also usually focuses on the pupils rather than on the nature of schooling, although there is a particular awareness of the parts that teachers and the curriculum play in the gender differentiation of schooling (e.g. Byrne, 1978; Deem, 1978; Delamont, 1980a; Evans, 1984c; Spender and Sarah, 1980). Very often social scientists study the victims of inequality rather than the perpetrators; this concentrates the policy makers' attention on alleviating inequalities through ameliorating the conditions of the victims, rather than by removing the causes. This approach is particularly tempting with children because there is a vain hope that by changing the conditions of the rising generation the inequalities will not be constructed again. However, such an approach ignores or disregards the structures and processes which, relatively unaffected, continue to produce the inequalities.

In relation to the part that schooling plays in gender inequalities, although there has been recognition of the importance of broader matters such as curriculum gender bias, teachers' perceptions etc., usually policy action is about changing children through their schooling, rather than changing the adults who continue to be sexist in their dealings with children. So, for example, the usual approach to dealing with the sex-segregated labour market (and higher levels of women's unemployment) is to encourage girls to 'broaden their options' to include 'non-traditional' jobs through career education, work experience, school-to-work transition programmes etc. However, it is less likely that sexist employment practices, sexism in the work place, sexist advertising, sexist toys, sexist parenting or sexist schooling are systematically addressed. Yet these are parts of the structures and processes which powerfully encourage boys and girls to be gender specific and gender 'appropriate' in their future lives. Such sexism is at the core of the gender order construction process.

Firkin suggests that, 'the forces of patriarchal society are resistant to change and, indeed, the development of new technology is in the process of forging a new patriarchal reality' (1983:2). If these contentions hold true, then the possibility of constructing, through schooling, a new generation with a relatively egalitarian gender order seems remote. In fact, for some authors on Australian primary schools (e.g. Bassett, Jacka and Logan, 1982), gender remains a matter unworthy of mention: this in spite of the researchers, teacher unions and educational bureaucracies who now address the topic. One expects that the continued invisibility of women, and of matters concerning gender in primary schooling, serves the shifting sands of patriarchy. Llewellyn (1980) and Davies (1984) point to similar invisibility in some of the more notable studies of schools and pupils (e.g. Hargreaves, 1967; Lacey, 1970; Willis, 1977).

Others recognise the significance of understanding gender as a feature of the workplace and careers of teachers, and have recorded and documented its effects (e.g. Acker, 1983; Byrne, 1978: 211–244; Deem, 1978:108–126; Sampson, 1983, 1986a). In some ways this literature is still concentrating on the victims of patriarchy, rather than on the perpetrators of it; the emphasis is now upon understanding women teachers and their subservient places within educational career structures. Acker criticises the sexist assumptions which have pervaded much of the research (by men) into teachers. She points to scholars 'twisting the meaning of some of the research findings' and concluding falsely about the supposed 'harm women do to the professional hopes of occupations' such as teaching (1983: 125). She finds problematic several conclusions from influential sociological studies, 'perhaps the most serious of which is their insistence that women's aspirations and family role responsibilities are sufficient explanations for their subordinate position in teaching' (p. 133).

Apple provides a different, but complementary, perspective when he argues that over the past twenty years 'the process of proletarianisation has had both a large and consistent effect' (1983:53). He asserts that teachers have experienced a declining control over their labour process: de-skilling, state fiscal crises and greater external control over their practice have all contributed to this. He notes that, without exception, those occupations which are most susceptible to proletarianisation are those predominantly occupied by women; something which may be due to, 'sexist practices of recruitment and promotion, the general tendency to care less about the conditions under which women labour (and) the way capital has historically colonised patriarchal relations' (1983:54). So for Apple, proletarianisation is a feature of contemporary capitalism that needs to be understood in terms of class and gender, and that affects teaching in those terms.

Women are in a majority in the teaching profession in Australia, yet a study of women teachers in the Education Department (now Ministry of Education) in Victoria found that the participation of women in the senior teaching and administrative positions had generally worsened since 1972, when many of the equal opportunity provisions were set in place. In the Victorian primary school division, which has about 80 per cent women employees, the percentage of women in senior positions dropped from 35 to 18 per cent during the period from 1973 to 1984. Women comprised about 60 per cent of the Education Department's teachers in 1984 but only occupied 17 per cent of the senior positions (Education Department of Victoria, Policy and Planning Unit, 1984). Sampson, in a national survey of a sample of teacher union members, uncovered a complicated pattern of characteristics and values for men and women teachers in relation to their careers and promotion. Whereas 51 per cent of women believed that they were discriminated against in pursuing a career, only 24 per cent of men believed that this was the case for women. The percentages were reversed when applications for promotion over the previous five years were analysed, with 24 per cent of women and 46 per cent of men applying. Thirty-eight per cent of men believed that their career was more important than their spouse's or partner's, a feeling held by only 8 per cent of women. However, 82 per cent of women believed that their career was at least equal in importance to their spouse's or partner's (Sampson, 1986).

A survey such as Sampson's, while it does have merits, is limited. It provides only the outlines of the nature and degree of gender division in the careers of teachers in Australia. This is part of the practical problem for social researchers who wish to study and explain the social processes which lead to the structural divisions in society. It is what some would call the problem of trying to link the processes of the 'micro' social world to the structures of the 'macro' society. Invariably, the research tools or methods, together with the underlying theory or methodology, of the one are inappropriate for the other. This brings us back to the narrative description of the race at Tordale school. In order to understand and explain that event, and its various individuals' motives and performances, it is necessary to see the race as a product of the school's activities, the structure of education in general, and of the broader structures of society, including gender.

Some matters of theory

The gender structures and processes that operate within primary school communities are the 'raw material' from which an emerging gender order is constructed. These social processes occur as a result of the interactive engagement of people with one another. In a primary school such engagement is usually at its most intense in the classroom, where as many as thirty or more people are confined for substantial periods of time, on most days of the week, for most weeks of the year. Each school class is a component of the school's structure, which itself engages with the general structure of schooling, the education system and of society at large. However, other contexts of engagement between people in primary schools—union meetings, school committees, the school council—have their interrelationships with the broader structures of society. These contexts interact with each other and the school class: sociologically, no school context can be understood as completely independent, fixed or simple.

One theoretical trap that beckons invitingly is to conceptualise the social processes and structures within the school as reflecting and reproducing those of the society of which it is a tiny fragment. Such determinist circularity should be avoided and we must recognise that social structures are just that: social, and that people, even primary school children, are able to influence their social worlds and play a part in constructing the structures which obtain. It seems commonsense, however, to recognise that they are neither free agents, nor all powerful in their capacity to shape their social worlds. The existing social structures, including those directly to do with primary schooling, have a shaping effect upon the social action people can take to shape similar structures in the future.

People's power, including that of school children, to shape their lives and that of others, is related to a variety of personal and cultural factors, including their deviousness, wit, aggressiveness, intelligence and guile, as well as their knowledge and experience. Knowledge, in this respect, is not in itself power, but is rather a 'fuel' which can be turned into power by those with the personal catalytic qualities (such as will), position and experience to do so. Hence, to control the dissemination of knowledge is to control a 'fuel supply' for power. However, one may see that both personal and cultural factors are shaped by social structural divisions, in particular, gender and class. Giddens (1979, 1981, 1984) has contributed substantially to the debate about human agency and social structure.

Writers about the transmission and structures of knowledge in schools have, not unreasonably, focused upon the curriculum, in both its formal and hidden forms, as the mechanism for such transmission and structures (e.g. Apple, 1971; Giroux and Purpel, 1983). The curriculum is seen as operated by, although not entirely constructed by, teachers upon their pupils. However, there are other structures of knowledge in schools which are more to do with how they operate as social organisations of both adults and children. I want to introduce the notion of *agenda* here because it emerged as a useful way of understanding some of the social processes that were recorded during the study and because it helps explain the theoretical orientation of the research. Such *agendas* may be seen as the structural framework for the operation of a hierarchical, bureaucratic and, to some extent, democratic organisation such as a school. These *agendas* extend beyond the simple statement of matters for discussion and debate within the informal and formal decision-making contexts of a school. Rather they resemble the tip of the cultural iceberg frozen from the sea of socially structured knowledge, values and beliefs which comprise the host society.

Individuals within a school have differing degrees of power to form and set the *agendas* for its operation. Their power may be seen to be derived from their position, for example, as principal, teacher, secretary, councillor or pupil; from their knowledge and experience; and from their personal capacities to exploit these positions in relation to others. Similarly, such power may be modified by the particular constraints or enhancement provided by others exercising their powers within the school and by the social class, gender, generation and ethnicity differentiation which obtain. Whether these people are male or female will affect not only the way they are able to use their positions, but also the processes through which they are able to attain such positions in the first place. It is probable that, in keeping with the gender-differentiated allocation of power in society, women occupying senior positions will find their ability to exploit such positions is more circumscribed than it is for men.

This research was designed to record the assembly of social structural components which both comprise and bear upon primary schools. Apple has stated that it is important to understand a school as an institution with its forms of knowledge and individual educators (1974:4). The research conformed to this approach, but with a particular focus on gender and the ways in which knowledge is structured in the pursuit of individual power.

2 The research project

The design and implementation of research projects requires researchers to negotiate a path between a variety of practical and theoretical obstructions. As Bell and Encel (1978) have shown, social researchers do not escape this challenge, and as Wild (1985) has explained, some even suffer as a consequence. It is often difficult to be precise about where the genesis of any particular research project rests and this is true for the present case. I had been involved in research in the area of gender and schooling for some years and as a consequence was invited to contribute to the National Seminar on the Education of Girls, which was held at Canberra in October 1982. The Commonwealth Schools Commission's Working Party on the Education of Girls organised the seminar as part of its preparation of a report to the Commission (1984). The inadequate amount of Australian research in the area was addressed at the National Seminar and was expressed in the report (1984:20-21). The working party had its own research budget within the Commission's Projects of National Significance scheme which it used to stimulate more Australian research. In early 1983 the working party advertised for applications for funding of research projects within its area of responsibility: the education of girls.

Getting going

A friend suggested that I apply for a Schools Commission grant because she believed that there was a need for more Australian school and classroom research of the kind I had done in primary schools and preschools. However, I knew that I had moved on in my thinking and research interests since those days. For me, the more I thought, read and taught about the relationship between gender, work, family life, and schooling, the more complex it became.

Together with a colleague, Daryl Nation, I studied a 'school-to-work' transition project for girls at a technical school in the Latrobe region of Victoria. This region provides most of the State's electricity from power stations fuelled by the vast, open cut, brown coal mines. Forestry, paper manufacture and farming are also important economic activities. Our involvement in this research project stimulated considerable thought and discussion about matters which were difficult to disentangle theoretically from one another. It was during this project that we read Williams's book, Open Cut, *and were impressed with her exposition of the relationships between family life, gender relations and work in a not dissimilar region. However, our research was more narrowly focused on technical schooling and the rising generation of women in the Latrobe region.*

The structure and nature of technical schooling, and of Valley Tech. itself, seemed to fit neatly with the proletarian and patriarchal nature of the population. Women teachers, especially those teaching Humanities subjects, did not fit very easily into the school. Neither did the girls themselves, where they comprised about a quarter of the students; nor were they going to fit very easily into the Latrobe region's labour force, where the junior female unemployment rate was about three times that for junior males.

Our interviews with the girls' families demonstrated that the parents, especially mothers, were interpreting their daughters's adult lives in a less traditionally gender differentiated way than they interpreted their own lives. Further, parents were attempting to influence and act towards their daughters in less traditionally differentiated ways. However, in many respects, the views and ideas they held and their capacities to act were shaped and limited by the broader social and economic structure of the Latrobe region.

As the Latrobe region steamed and smoked its way into the twenty-first century, its women were becoming increasingly marginalised as the cycle of manual construction work, followed by technical maintenance and supervision work, rolled its way around the region's electricity generation, mining and other industrial projects. This raised the question for me of whether a primary school classroom study would contribute to understanding the broader social processes and structures which form Valley life and also help inform a more general understanding of primary schooling in Australia? I soon dismissed the idea of focusing purely on classroom life and moved on to think in terms of a study that looked at primary schools as (mostly paid) work environments for adults and (unpaid) work environments for children. The ways in which gender shaped these two aspects was central to the project. My previous research led me to conclude that it was important to understand a school in relation to its local community and its pupils' families.

It was at this point that the practical constraints of my own life began to shape the project. I was limited by the location and nature of my work and by my own relatively recent parenthood. I was teaching at a regional College of Advanced Education during a period when the conventional wisdom in Canberra, which flowed swiftly through to the college's management, was that contract employment, especially with its usual lack of study leave, superannuation and other normal employment conditions for tenured academic staff, was the panacea for all tertiary educational ills. I was one of many of the recently appointed contract staff who was beavering away at both on and off campus teaching in the pursuit of a life in academia. Research and publication is not generally seen as important in the work of a college academic, whereas the opposite is the case in a university. However, this difference was diminishing, especially when it came to appointing new staff, when the colleges cheerfully selected those with the best research and publication record. The problem for contract staff is how to start the job, plan a research project, execute it and endeavour to publish before the end of a contract, whilst also doing a good teaching job. Assuming the contract is long enough, and I was 'lucky' with three years, it should just be possible with extra work at evenings and weekends.

For me, the possibility of a research grant, whilst attracting additional responsibilities and constraints, had the advantage of enabling me to engage a research assistant to help with the fieldwork. In the event, this not only reduced the time I had to spend in the field, but also provided greater flexibility: we shifted our research commitments to match our respective parental and my work commitments, and we could also cover two simultaneous events when necessary. The guidelines for the Commonwealth Schools Commission's Projects of National Significance included requirements about the duration, contexts and scope of proposed research projects, which also affected the final design of the project. Most notably, the extent to which families could be included in the research was limited to those who had children at the schools. My feeling was that a broader view of a school community would have been better for studying the relationships between the structural and process features of schools and the society at large.

I also believed it was important for me to try to give the people being studied any information that might be useful to them. Our experience with the technical schools' transition project for girls was that my report Girls and jobs: improving the odds *and Daryl Nation's television documentary had proved useful for the people involved. Although we nursed some reservations about the impact of our media and their messages on our audiences, I decided to produce a report for each school as part of the project. These reports were aimed to help the general school adult community understand the ways in which gender structured the life of their school and, where possible, offer ideas and suggestions for change toward a more egalitarian education in this respect. Such changes were amongst the policies of the Australian and most state governments of the day and were in line with the Commonwealth Education Commission's (1983) guidelines.*

In early 1983 I submitted my research proposal. It was accepted and the practical demands of the project became a feature of my life for over a year. During this period, like so many other contract staff, I continued to scan the academic appointment columns of the papers for more secure employment. Because of my commitment to research I wished to return to working in a university and in 1984 I took an appointment at Deakin University in Geelong. Both my present and previous employers were cooperative in enabling the research project to continue smoothly. However, some ideas I had for follow-up work in the schools after the reports had been distributed had to be jettisoned. Apart from some occasional contacts with people in the school communities, I, like so many other social researchers, moved on to new pastures.

Research methods

It was necessary to develop a methodology that would enable a broad understanding of the schools and their communities, but that also permitted the recording of the everyday negotiation and social construction of gender. A pluralistic approach was adopted, embracing the analysis of census data from the local collection districts, through to the ethnographic study of particular social contexts. The need to focus upon the nature of gender in the schools meant that the entire methodology needed to contain a gender-critical perspective. Such a view would also serve to ensure that the research did not exist in an atheoretical vacuum, a criticism which has been levelled at positivist and interpretive sociological perspectives alike (Angus, 1985:22).

Selection of schools

The nature of, and resources available for, the project dictated that two primary schools be studied simultaneously during the year. It was decided to select one 'town school' and one 'rural school' in the Latrobe region. The schools selected were broadly representative of Australian schools of their type in terms of size and location. Because the schools were to be studied simultaneously, pairs of schools were chosen which were within a practicable travelling distance by car from each other. Two pairs of schools were shortlisted and, prior to submitting the research proposal, the principals of one pair of schools were approached and asked if their schools would be willing to be involved. The remaining pair were not to be approached unless one or both of the first pair of principals declined to participate in the project. Both of the first principals, Rod Miles from Tordale primary school and Ted Symes from Linfield primary school, agreed to be involved.

After the project was accepted by the Commission, the school staffs and councils were given an outline of the proposed study and were met by the author to discuss the research. In each school there was both interest and a general willingness to cooperate in the project. Each individual's confidentiality was assured within the limitations of providing a report for each school, whereby particular people, especially at Tordale which is a more intimate community, could be identified.

The fieldwork

We immediately commenced the fieldwork on receiving confirmation of approval of the project. We studied the schools across two school years, from the last term of 1983 and into 1984. The majority of the fieldwork was completed by the middle of 1984, although some small pieces of work occurred during the remainder of the year. We were granted the freedom to be in the schools and to attend as many meetings, school camps, excursions etc. as we felt was necessary.

The fieldwork comprised a variety of data collection methods including: the analysis of census figures, school records and school, community and government documents; the observation and recording of meetings, classes and other school activities; and the interviewing of teachers, parents, pupils and other significant people. Appendix 9.1 provides details of our research methods.

Reflection

I often find it difficult to write about the research methods I have employed on a project. I think it is because the research planning is made with the limitations of foresight and the writing completed with the benefit of hindsight. It is hindsight which sees the strengths, weaknesses and problems which beset a research programme.

In general, things went very smoothly with this project. However, it seemed initially that our work was going to be frustrated by a series of events which conspired against us. The travel budget looked likely to be depleted by the end of 1983, only three months into the project, due to 'circumstances beyond our control'. The first indication occurred before the project had officially started when Ted Symes, the principal at Linfield primary school, mentioned that the staff and parents were to hold a residential, three day workshop to plan the school's new social studies curriculum. The workshop commenced on a Saturday in a pleasant rural school camp about forty kilometres from Linfield. Rosemary and I were invited to attend and I was also asked to talk about the research project for a few minutes during the first day. As one might expect, the opportunity was a wonderful one for the research and between us we attended for the three days. The travel budget was reduced in these three days by an amount which should have lasted for a few weeks.

The tragic 'Ash Wednesday' bushfires also had an unexpected effect on our research and the travel budget. Due to the dangerous fire conditions prevailing at the beginning of 1983, the Education Department withdrew or refused approval for many school camps and activities which involved travelling to rural areas. This meant that large schools such as Linwood postponed their camps programme from the beginning to the end of the year, when the weather would again be suitable to take young children away. Therefore, during the first three months of the project there were some school camps that we felt it was important to attend and observe and often the teachers we wished to interview were away at camps or were covering for colleagues at camp during the 'non-contact' periods when we had hoped to interview them. Again the travel budget was being expended more rapidly than planned and also the interviews were running behind schedule. Fortunately, 1984 began with everything falling into place and the project returned to schedule. Some adjustments were made to enable the remaining travel costs to be met.

The Linfield parent-teacher workshop represents an example of events and meetings that inevitably arose as a result of chance occurrences during the course of our study. It was often necessary to make quick decisions about whether to observe such events on the basis of their pertinence to the project. In general, if in doubt, we erred on the side of making an observation so that potentially useful evidence was not missed. However, this does raise the practical and theoretical matter of where a social scientist engaged in this type of project should fix the spatial, temporal and other structural boundaries of the study.

Towards the end of the fieldwork it became difficult to decide when to stop systematically observing, interviewing and collecting material about the schools; there seemed to be no natural break: school life just carried on. School holidays were used by certain adults as an opportunity to work on the agenda *for the next term, indeed some of our most useful interviews took place during school holidays when people were interested in spending most of a morning or afternoon talking about themselves and their work. In the end the fieldwork gradually decreased as the need to analyse the data dominated, but particular matters of concern to the project were pursued several weeks after the majority of the fieldwork had been completed. If, as I said at the beginning of this chapter, it is difficult to point to the genesis of some social research projects, it can also be difficult to recognise the exodus.*

In another respect I had set a limit on the research which I now believe was unnecessary. This concerned the interviews with the pupils. As was discussed previously, in order to minimise the hesitation that the pupils, especially the younger ones, may have had about talking to an interviewer who wanted to tape-record everything they said, I decided to use small group interviews. While this was successful as a method, it became clear that most pupils would have been fairly comfortable in an appropriate individual interview context. Subsequently, I have read Ochiltree and Amato's work with the Institute of Family Studies in which children were interviewed about their family lives. This work confirms my view that we could have improved our research, perhaps by conducting a sequence of individual interviews after the group interviews. In this way we may have obtained more detailed information about matters such as the gender division of domestic and breadwinning labour, the pupils' perceptions of gender and their interpretations of their schools.

My final reflection concerns the need for the research design to be reflexively gender-critical. From the outset the notion of me as the male 'research director' and Rosemary as the female 'research assistant' was problematic. It seemed that a research project that was to adopt a gender critical perspective of schooling needed to also be gender critical of itself in order to fulfil its purpose. I could see that our lives intersected at that particular point partly because of the ways in which gender had structured our biographies, especially in terms of our breadwinning and domestic work. We recognised that our particular gender positions were useful in conducting this particular research, in other words we were saying that two men or two women researchers would be unable to do the research as satisfactorily. As the research progressed we had many discussions about the ways in which gender had a bearing upon our explanation of the particular data. The processes involved in these discussions often demonstrated a more highly critical awareness of the activities and sayings of the people of our own sex, than of the opposite sex. So, for example, I was often likely to see an aspect of man's behaviour as indicative of his masculine intentions to dominate, and Rosemary would recognise evidence of a woman's particular intention to be submissive. Although, of course, on occasions we perceived things similarly and on others the cross-sex perceptions were sharper.

In another practical way the sex of the researchers was important. We found that in some circumstances it was important to organise our interviews so that we interviewed our own sexes. It is impossible to substantiate, but it seemed clear that some men and women were likely to be more frank with interviewers of the same sex than of the opposite sex. Claire Williams in her study of a Queensland mining community reached a similar conclusion which helped us make our decisions. Since the research, I have read Ann Oakley's feminist critique of interviewing and David Morgan's discussion of masculinity and sociological inquiry, both of which stimulate a deeper critical reflection.

We deliberately took sex into consideration for our observation of some meetings and activities. For example, we felt that Rosemary would be the most successful observer of Tordale mothers' club. However, in most respects we shared the fieldwork on the basis of the practical aspects of our work. On some occasions we both attended meetings or events, which provided some useful reference points for our comparative analysis and explanation.

When the project was over we went our separate ways in the pursuit of our work: Rosemary to help develop an advice and resource centre for working women and I to continue as an aca-demic and to write this book. In different ways, the things we learned and experienced at Linfield and Tordale continue to affect our work.

Part 1 The adults' world of school

3 The school councils

Adults have always been instrumental in the development and operation of schools and education systems. They have often had some formal status as advisory committees, boards of governors, management committees, parents and citizens organisations etc., but their powers and responsibilities have often been limited. In essence, governments have maintained control over schools through bureaucracies and agencies, with certain individuals, especially school principals, being delegated considerable power and responsibility over their individual schools.

For about a century, and especially over the past two to three decades, Australian school systems have expanded, due to population increases, extensions to the ages of compulsory schooling and the greater emphasis on the completion of secondary schooling. Simultaneously, the operation of school systems has become more centralised and bureaucratic. In contemporary Victoria, local school folklore has become replete with stories about 'the Department' and its various bungles, delays and intransigence. By the early 1970s schooling had become a regular topic on the political agenda in Victoria as separate interests tried to exert their influence over educational policy, practice and expenditure. Problems over staff shortages (the Education Department resorted to chartering Qantas aircraft to transport hundreds of teachers from the U.S.A. and Britain), examinations, migrant education, curriculum control, alternative schools, school accommodation and equipment etc., all served to make life difficult for 'the Department'.

By the early 1970s, there were three teachers' unions, each representing one of the Education Department's three school divisions: primary, secondary and technical. The history of these three teacher unions shows periods of wrangling and squabbling within the antecedent unions, and with the Education Department and governments of the time. Arguably, this history helped to set the scene for the massive reorganisation of the administration of education in Victoria which was to follow (Bessant and Spaull, 1972; Frazer, Dunstan and Creed, 1985; Spaull and Hince, 1986).

By 1979 the Government had steeled itself for a widespread restructuring of the Education Department, from its upper echelons through to school councils and the classroom itself. After his appointment as Minister of Education, Alan Hunt set in train a review process, ostensibly to formulate aims and objectives, together with the strategies, structures and administrative organisation to fulfil them (Hunt, 1985). The reaction of the three teacher unions, together with other commentators, left one with the view that the restructuring was as much about curbing the unions as it was about moulding the Education Department into an efficient administrative enterprise. Bates (1984) has discussed the changes during this period in terms of the metaphors and rhetoric abounding in the various ministerial statements, policy documents, 'green' and 'white' papers etc. Bates argues that, 'Education systems, . . . are . . . a physical working out of the cultural metaphors and myths held by educators and administrators. Moreover, these cultural artifacts are shaped by the rhetoric, symbols and metaphors that are operating in the wider society' (1984:5).

The contradictions, conflicts and tensions which littered the rhetoric and the policy decisions of the time were to find their way into the everyday life of Linfield and Tordale primary schools. In particular, the rhetoric surrounding the devolution of power from a centralised Education Department to regional and local centres (schools) abraded harshly against the actual concentration of power over policy decisions at the point where political and departmental bosses met. By 1982, when the Liberal Party lost government in Victoria to the Labor Party for the first time in nearly a quarter of a century, the primary, secondary and technical school divisions had been abolished, the senior positions in the Education Department had been spilled, regional education offices had been fortified with new staff and the three teacher unions had cooperated in opposition to staffing and other changes as never before.

In many respects the Labor governments since that time have continued in much the same vein. There have been some variations to the rhetoric—the desirability of 'participation' has informed much of the change to school councils—and the relationship with the unions has usually been more cooperative than under previous state governments. The move toward a centralised curriculum called *Frameworks* (1985), to apply from preschool through to the end of secondary school, the revamping of secondary education in the wake of the *Blackburn Report* (1985), and the abolition, in 1986, of the Education Department in favour of a new corporate-styled Ministry of Education, all smacked of tight political control, despite the rhetoric about consultation and local participation.

School councils were one of the first targets of change after the change of government in 1982. Within Labor's first year of office there had been a series of ministerial papers on education, the fourth of which concerned school councils (1983). This paper made several enticing claims:

> School councils will have major responsibility for deciding the educational policies of their schools...
>
> This increase in (educational policy) responsibilities of councils will be of fundamental significance.
>
> To enable this school-based policy development to be democratically representative, the legislation will provide for council membership to be...parents, teachers and, where appropriate, students...
>
> The provisions on membership will give formal expression to the Government's belief that the most effective educational program depends on a process of consultation and negotiation among those vitally affected, so that the policies adopted will reflect their values and goals, thus increasing the prospect of wholehearted support (1983:5-6).

These initial statements suggested that the changes would result in 'consultation among those vitally affected' and lead to each school developing its own educational policies and programmes commensurate with the school community's values and goals. This assumes several things, but particularly it rests on two beliefs: that there is a consensus of values and goals in each school community which can be discerned, represented and articulated through its school council members; and that each school community's values and goals are good ones for its children. However, the Government was not so naive as perhaps its rhetoric would suggest. Later in Ministerial Paper Number 4 boundaries for schools' educational policy-making are explained. For example, it made clear that central control is not being relinquished and that both central and regional offices will give school councils 'support...to assist' their work. It is stated clearly that:

> The fact that the Government is deliberately departing from a tradition of centralised policy control should not be interpreted as moving to the opposite extreme of absolute local control.

> It is the Government's philosophy that the achievement of desirable State-wide educational and social goals requires a number of broad, but firm, State policy guidelines. To take a simple example, school council involvement in educational policy determination will *not* give a school council the option of asking the school staff to ignore the Government's multicultural, nonsexist or such other policies (original emphasis) (1983:6).

In other words, school councils were free to determine the educational policies of their schools as long as they concurred with the centrally determined policy. In addition, the Government said each new school council would be accountable, not only in the 'financial sense', but also as 'the mechanism [for increasing]...the strength of the relationship between each school and its community...to increase each school's accountability to the community' (1983:8). Accountability was also to have another feature:

> The essence of the change in the role of the school council is that it makes the principal and staff educationally accountable directly to the school community rather than to distant departmental senior officers. Councils will not have delegated authority which may be overruled by appeals to the centre; they will have authority in their own right (1983:9).

Given that school councillors are elected volunteers, except for the principal who is an *ex-officio* member, the responsibilities imposed on them are fairly onerous. Indeed, more recently the Government proposed and then rejected even wider school council responsibilities for staffing, budget management and educational policy. However, in practice, school councils negotiated their role within the parameters defined in Ministerial Working Paper Number 4 and by the Education Department (Amendment) Regulations 1984 (Amendment No. 60). These regulations spelt out the legal detail of the new school councils' elections, powers and responsibilities. They further demarcated the boundaries of school councils' work, for example, they defined the methods of employing ancillary staff and prevented councils from owning real estate. However, the notion that the teaching staff and the principal would be 'educationally accountable' to the school community through the school council looked dangerously close to eroding the professional scope of teachers.

The membership of the new school councils is outlined in Ministerial Paper Number 4 and, for primary schools, at least half must be parents and no more than a half must be teachers. The school's principal is a voting member of the school council. Also, up to one fifth of the total membership of a school council may be coopted, 'to represent wider community interests' (1983:9). However, the school's teachers are excluded from cooption. Within these provisions each existing school council amended its constitution, which was then ratified and made into a Constituting Order for approval by the Governor in Council. The new school councils commenced in 1984 on the 1st April—April Fool's Day!—a date which now applies each year for the handover of one school council to the next.

The making of the 1984 Tordale and Linfield primary school councils

The established farming families of Tordale retained the typical rural suspicion of the 'pollies' in parliament. Some of them were relatively wealthy in terms of their land ownership if not income, however most are the remnants of the rural working class in the area. With a new Labor government intent on making changes to Tordale school council their cynicism about metropolitan authority was quickly rekindled. Rod Miles knew that, as principal, he was responsible for enacting such changes. In his few years at the school he had learned how to deal with Tordale people. He presents himself conservatively; he looks and dresses older than his years, he is a keen church-goer and he is a Vietnam veteran. He also has a sharp mind and reaches firm opinions which he presents convincingly. His strategy was to suggest that the changes were merely formalising something that was happening already at Tordale and that it would give the council more responsibility for its own affairs. The wider powers over curriculum policy and the requirement to have teachers on the council were not emphasised. The existing council had ten parents and the principal as an *ex-officio* member. The school's three teachers were able to attend any council meeting, but they rarely did so, and none attended during our research at the school.

The more recent Tordale families—referred to as 'Blockies' by the farmers because they often lived on 'blocks' of a few hectares in area—were mostly members of the emerging middle class who worked in the nearby towns and industries. They were less concerned about the school council changes: some saw these as in their own interests and others saw them as less than significant because they believed that parents' new powers would be circumscribed by the government anyway. Cynthia Jasper, a lively member of the school community, said of the people who, at the end of 1983, were lobbying for a place on the new council that, 'They think they are going to have supreme power. They're not. I mean we all know what they are going to have. But they see a few things on the ABC and read the *Age* and think "we can hire and fire staff, and work out curriculum". I think that's why they're interested.'

The primary school in Tordale is the main focus for the community. To be on the school council is a symbol of one's influence in the community. It was rare for more than one or two absences at the school council's monthly meetings. At the end of 1983 there were 36 families sending their children to the school and the lobbying for the seven parent positions on the newly constituted 1984 council was discreetly intense. In addition, the mothers' club—an interesting anachronism—could elect two members and the three teachers, in effect, had to elect each other to fill the three teacher vacancies.

Democracy in action

It was lunchtime. Donna Morton bounded into the staffroom with an armful of books, apparently in a gregarious and carefree mood. Today was a good day. Rod Miles smiled as Donna entered the tiny staffroom cum office. Now everyone was present he could get them to fill out their council nominations. Donna Morton set the tone by announcing that dire consequences would befall her two colleagues, Stephanie Bell and Carmel Walls, if they did not propose and second her nomination. So, the three teachers, in between the nibbling of crispbread biscuits and the chewing of sandwiches, put on a farcical display of mutual nominating and seconding. No lobbying required here; everyone duly elected.

The parents' nominations were causing concern for Rod Miles. Certainly, he had received nominations from some of the 'sensible' parents he liked, but there were a few others, particularly Karen Hersch and Cynthia Jasper, whom he could well do without. He hadn't forgotten the trouble he had been caused by some of these parents, mostly mothers, over the health and human relationships curriculum. Karen Hersch also had the advantage over him of being the driving force behind the highly successful annual fun run. This event provided many thousands of dollars for the school's coffers, but also, until he managed to moderate it, gave people like Karen Hersch more influence in the school than he would have wished.

Rod Miles's solution, under the guise of participatory democracy, was to encourage other parents to nominate. In this way there was plenty of competition against Karen Hersch and Cynthia Jasper. All that remained was to undermine their support. An opportunity arose one day when Martin Dewey, a 'sensible' parent, telephoned the school. Rod Miles moved swiftly and smoothly:

Right, yes, well, now Martin, while you're on the phone, about the school council elections. Have you thought of standing? Because we could do with someone like you, what with the new building extensions we're going to need sorting out this year. . . .

Well, the nominations are going quite well, but we feel you'd be the sort of person, don't get me wrong, but we need a balance of people . . .

I see, well think about it, it would be good if you could give it a go . . .

Later in the conversation Karen Hersch's nomination was mentioned:

Don't get me wrong. I'm not saying that she hasn't done a lot for the school. We all know that, what with the fun run and all, she has been terrific, really terrific. But she's a bit pushy, which helped get people moving over the fun run, but will upset some of the sorts of people we have on the council. That's all I'm saying. It's not just me though, there are others, I'm just expressing their views.

Election day was March 14 1984. The meeting was organised by Rod Miles in one of the classrooms at the school. By this time his strategy was beginning to bear fruit. Martin Dewey had nominated, which made ten nominees for the seven positions. The mothers' club had already elected their two representatives. Some of the first parents arrived as Rod Miles organised the final seating and election arrangements. Carmel Walls and her husband were in the school staffroom preparing to act as tellers. With five minutes to go to the start of the meeting about fifteen parents had arrived, some were sitting and talking, others were standing outside the room either talking or settling their children down to watch a video in another classroom. By 8pm about 25 parents were seated and Rod Miles was standing at the front smiling and talking aloud to groups of parents. He used the opportunity to display the plan of, and reinforce the idea of the need for, the proposed extension to the school. He hoped the new council would approve the idea and finance it, largely through its fun run income.

Within a few minutes the number of parents had risen to 36. The late-comers were either squashing into the odd vacant seats or were scouring the school for any available adult-sized seats. A few parents resorted to sitting on desks or cupboards. It was a warm, humid evening and in the crowded classroom the air became heavy with human odour and the noise of different conversations. Rod Miles stood at the front of the meeting and was anxious to start the meeting. He spoke loudly and a little nervously:

Can I start the meeting? Thanks. Thanks everyone for attending, it really is a good turn out. I don't envisage it being a long meeting.

> *Regional office have sent me a whole book of procedures for this meeting. I'm not going to do quite a few things set down in the booklet because, quite frankly, three-quarters of them are ridiculous. Can I have someone as a minutes secretary? I was going to suggest one of the mothers' club reps. No? Yes? Oh great. Thanks Jane.*

The principal continued the meeting by thanking the council for their efforts during the year. He then mentioned the nature of the changes to school councils and noted particularly that there were now three elected staff on the new council, 'something which other schools have had since 1976'. He explained the voting procedure and distributed the ballot papers. However, due to the unexpected number of people at the meeting, there were insufficient ballot papers and another six were photocopied. The muffled sound of the children's video programme was all that could be heard as people voted; even the principal, unknowingly contrary to the regulations, voted as a parent.

While Carmel Walls and her husband counted the votes, Rod Miles invited questions and discussion. A father asked if teacher or mothers' club representatives could be nominated as president, secretary or treasurer, by the new council members. Rod Miles, ignoring the question of teachers, replied that the mothers' club representatives could be nominated and elected 'if it is the will of the council'. A father at the back of the room protested, saying he had 'raised this matter in the past' about fathers being excluded from the mothers' club and, therefore, from electing or standing as representatives. He was doubly angry now that mothers' club representatives could become office bearers. Another father gruffly added support to the complainant and others began to grumble amongst themselves.

Rod Miles adeptly changed the subject by raising the matter of the new school buildings. This topic is one which was close to the hearts of many of the parents and, not the least, with the principal himself. It was quickly seized upon. Rod Miles was asked if 'he is happy with the present school buildings?' He needed no further prompting:

> No I'm not. In fact I'm very unhappy about it. In fact I'd be prepared to say that no-one here would live in this building. When people come to the school they see it as a school and not as any other public building. If it were seen like any other public building it would probably be condemned. . . Private schools get a better deal. I believe the provision of buildings for State schools is abysmal.

Rod Miles had been campaigning, mostly covertly, about the condition of the school buildings for some time. The accumulated capital in the school accounts, mostly from the fun run proceeds, gave him the opportunity to solve the problem in spite of the Education Department's refusal to help. He used the opportunity of the election meeting to shape the *agenda* for the new school council, where he could also depend on the three teachers' votes. One of the main barriers was the cost which, in spite of the school's reserves, was beyond its immediate means. Rod Miles told the parents that:

> Either of the two projects will be within the capacity of this community. You will probably have to float some kind of loan or something. Otherwise, by the time you have saved up you will find the cost has gone up astronomically through inflation. . . That's a council decision. I will work like a dog on anything the council comes up with.

Carmel Walls entered the room to give Rod Miles the results of the election. By now he had succeeded in starting to shape the *agenda* by giving the future council members—all of whom were at the meeting—details about the building project.

In a small community like Tordale, elections can be intense and embarrassing affairs. Everyone knew that three nominees would not be elected and that their names would be common knowledge. Furthermore, for the one year only, the half of the elected members with the most votes would serve for two years, the remaining half for one year. This enabled half the council to be elected in the following, and subsequent, years for two-year terms. Thus, the council elections became three tiered popularity polls: the most popular received two years, the least popular none and those in the middle one.

Silence prevailed as the principal read out the names and wrote them down on the blackboard, starting with the four parents who would serve two years. Two women and two men, including John Sheriff the past president, received two-year terms. Two men and one woman—Karen Hersch, who was to endure a difficult and occasionally bitter time on council—received one year terms. Cynthia Jasper was not elected. Office bearers were elected by the new members: John Sheriff was returned unopposed as president; Daphne Wearing and Martin Dewey were elected unopposed as treasurer and secretary respectively. There were eight women and five men on the 1984 school council, including the teachers. In 1983, with no teachers, the balance was equal, however, as we shall see later in this chapter, the equality did not extend to the council's practice. But, let us now see how Linfield school coped with its election process.

Democracy in apathy

The Linfield primary school council's annual general meeting was held on March 19 1984. As usual, the venue was the staff room, with the members seated around the tables nested together near the centre of the room, where most staff ate their lunches and discussed the affairs of the day. If even one tenth of the 550 or more parents and the 25 teachers had attended the meeting, the staffroom would have been filled to overflowing. However, everyone knew that even one per cent of the parents and teachers would have been cause for surprise and celebration. No-one was surprised, although there was a celebration of sorts, complete with cask wine, but not much cheese because Brian Garden, the president, had left it at home. The celebration was more to do with recognising the council's and others' efforts during what had been a taxing year. The proposed relocation, and possible integration, of the local Special Developmental School (SDS) for intellectually disabled children within Linfield primary school was a major issue for the council. It involved a lot of work and progress was elusive.

Seven people attended this, the final, meeting for the 1983 council. The principal and two staff representatives were present and four of the parents, including the president. Two parents and one teacher were absent from the meeting, and there remained one unfilled parent vacancy. There was a general air of resigned acceptance that the many important matters to be reported at the AGM were to pass by without anyone outside of the council even knowing about them, let alone debating them. The council's monthly meetings were often long affairs of three hours or more. Over the past three months there had been several extra council meetings over the SDS issue. These people had given a lot of time to the school council and, quite apart from the lack of recognition, there were no others volunteering to do their bit. Apathy reigned and it reigned hard!

The problem was: who was going to take over the enlarged and more powerful 1984 school council. Ted Symes, the principal, reluctantly admitted that he had only received one parent nomination, from an existing council member, for the seven positions. The teachers had organised themselves, mainly through the local subbranch of the VTU, into nominating their seven people. To add to Ted Symes' woes, one parent council member was leaving the town, and Brian Garden was unable to continue as president. During the course of discussion three other parents said that, in the circumstances, they would re-nominate for the new school council. Brian Garden believed that the tasks of a council member were becoming even more onerous under the new regulations. He reflected ruefully, 'Although it's important to be democratic, in fact, we really need to be more selective in our school council members, so that they will be capable of handling the job'.

Everyone agreed to try and hunt for more nominees. Events were to prove them unsuccessful. At the close of nominations three days later, the only nominees were those four indicated at the meeting. There was not to be a packed and tense election meeting for Linfield school; no meeting was called.

At almost eight o'clock, the time the AGM was due to start, Brian Garden adjourned the final meeting for the 1983 council. He arose from his seat and announced he was to, 'go and see if there are any parents who are coming to attend the AGM . . . I might get a hell of a shock one day and find some parents outside.' He returned three minutes later. He was not suffering from shock.

The new Linfield school council failed to reach its full complement of parent representatives. The principal, following the regulations, called for nominations a second time and obtained just one further nominee. The nominees were declared elected and the new school council went into operation with four women and eight men.

The contrasts between Tordale and Linfield schools are, as one can see, quite marked. At Tordale there was consistent and vigorous parent and community involvement in the school; at Linfield there was minimal involvement. Tordale school was the focus for the local community; Linfield school was merely a feature in the town's landscape. Tordale had more women than men on the council; Linfield had the opposite. Tordale had minimal staff activity on the council; Linfield had substantial staff activity. In addition, Tordale was an emerging middle-class rural community whereas Linfield was sustaining its working-class milieu. In spite of these and other contrasts, one similarity they shared was the Government's changes to school councils. These two schools were not selected for study on the basis of their dissimilarities, but because they represented typical small rural and large town schools, respectively, in Australia. Although there were degrees of variation, other local schools experienced similar changeovers to the new school councils. Indeed, the inverse relationship between size of school and degree of parental involvement, seems uncannily clear. At Tordale and Linfield, there was little impact on parental or community involvement in the schools, although one could argue that the legislative and compositional changes are only the beginning of the process.

Case studies of council issues

The following three case studies are centred on significant issues pursued by the two school councils during 1983. The part that gender plays in shaping the decision-making processes of these peak deliberative structures emerges as part of the broader *gender agenda* of the communities and society.

The ride-on mower

Tordale school possessed a large self-propelled mower which was used by parents to cut the extensive areas of grass. On October 5 1983, John Sheriff raised the matter of the grass-cutting because it was his responsibility to organise the maintenance of the grounds. Ten members attended the meeting, nine of whom were parents, six women and three men, and the principal. The meeting was held, as usual, in a school classroom. The president and secretary sat next to one another at the teacher's desk, facing the council members, who sat at the pupils' desks. The principal sat apart from the rest at the desk to the side of the classroom which was turned to face into the room.

After two hours the matter of the purchase of a ride-on mower was introduced under general business. John Sheriff explained the problems with the present mower, but had not got beyond mentioning starting and cutting blade problems, before a humorous interjection was made by one of the male members of council. The other male parent present joined in and soon the president found himself the butt of their jokes. These two men were Tordale farmers, whereas the president worked in the operations division of a local industry—he was a Blockie. The farmers joked that the president wanted a ride-on mower to play with at weekends; a ride-on mower was seen as a symbol of rural, middle-class, Blockie life.

The Farmers believed the old machine should be used, or one of them could cut the grass with a tractor. John Sheriff insisted that the old machine was difficult to use and maintain, and that a tractor was unsuitable for some areas of the grounds. He reasoned that a ride-on mower is a more attractive machine to use and, therefore, obtaining volunteers to cut the grass would be easier. Rod Miles supported this view, but questioned whether a ride-on mower would be suitable for the grass. This was a typical response from the principal in such circumstances, he was having an 'each way' bet. Now the levity had ceased and the president was making headway. The men agreed that he should investigate the matter further; the women did not contribute.

As members arrived for the November meeting the president distributed sales pamphlets for different ride-on mowers. People casually perused them before, and occasionally during, the council meeting. Nine members attended, five women and four men. An hour into the meeting, John Sheriff raised the matter of the mower. Discussion followed about the practical qualities of different machines and the deals they could expect from local retailers. The principal talked about sales tax exemption and the likely second hand value when they eventually sold the machine. The conversation drifted off the topic and meandered through anecdotes about the merits of various retailers, grasscutting, slashers and cows. The men did all the talking about mowers; the women initially remained silent, but when the men waxed anecdotal, they held a completely different discussion in the back row. Eventually, the president brought discussion back to the topic and, although no final decision was made, it was understood that about $2500 would be spent on a mower.

There were five women and four men present at the December meeting. Mid-way through the meeting the mower purchase was raised by the president. He presented further details about costs and reminded everyone that they had been considering it for some months and a decision ought to be made. The principal spoke about the financial implications and concluded that the purchase seemed worthwhile. After fifteen minutes it was decided to purchase a new mower. The discussion had focused on the technical features of the competing machines and on the financial arrangements. The men completely accounted for the former discussion, and the latter was shared between men and women. The president dominated the debate about the technical features and the principal dominated the debate about finances.

The school council was able to consider spending $2500 on a ride-on mower—which represents $33 for each pupil—because of its relative wealth. This wealth is accrued annually through the Tordale fun run which some local women initiated a few years ago and which has been substantially run by women ever since. Therefore, John Sheriff was able to press for the purchase of expensive mowing machinery because the women had filled the school council's coffers. There was never any recognition during the school council debates on the matter that this was the case.

The health and human relationships curriculum

The previous case centres on an inanimate object clearly within the council's purview. The present case is centred on sexual and human relationships, includes family nutrition and parenting, and touches on the tensions between teachers and parents, and between the class interests of the Blockies and the Farmers.

It is difficult to discern when health and human relationships became an issue at Tordale. Several incidents in the latter half of 1983 stimulated discussions amongst the teachers, the mothers' club and the school council. However, the driving force was Janet Waters, Blockie, and president of the mothers' club. She said that the issue started,

> . . . because I could see that we had a group of sixth graders last year who seemed to me to be fairly mature kids. It seemed to me to be a good idea to run a programme of some sort whereby the kids would begin to respect themselves and each other as being male and females. . . Girls weren't getting any respect from boys as girls, and the girls weren't deserving it either. . . We (the mothers' club) also wanted to give some sort of body awareness programme, have the kids helped by someone in an expert field in basic sex education. They could have another figure, another person, if their questions weren't being answered at home. . . Grooming and language, their language is atrocious. . . We felt that they needed some help before they were confronted with 150 year sevens next year. They needed someone to come and help.
>
> I felt that we, as mothers, needed some help too. Mothers, because they are more readily available during the day. And we were thinking of something at the school. Dads too, of course, I'm not that old fashioned. We didn't do very much, other than work out what we really wanted.

Janet Waters' statement is replete with symbols of the tensions which surrounded the issue at the school. Her views were a mixture of middle-class conservatism and liberalism. She saw a need for 'experts' to supplement the teachers, she believed that the parents—and here she was placing the responsibility at the feet of the mothers—were not sufficiently capable of informing their children about sexuality and she thought the children's language and grooming were 'atrocious'. Using the mothers' club she managed to 'work out what we really wanted' and transmit this to the school council, staff and principal.

Although the focus was the health and human relationships curriculum at the school, this was also being used as a vehicle for other worries. Janet Waters expressed concerns about the lack of supervision of children in the school grounds at lunchtimes, she felt this enabled the bad behaviour and language to proliferate. She was upset at the nutritional guidance given in class and by the mothers' club who offered, 'rotten, old saveloys (provided for sale by the mothers' club for lunch on winter Fridays)...You're giving them this over-preserved, over-processed, plastic junk and then expecting them to spend the next half day learning'.

She was mortified to find that the children did not share her concerns. One Friday, when Janet Waters replaced the saveloys with some of her own, home-made, vegetable soup she discovered that, 'some of the kids had thrown it down the gully trap'!

With any issue that is being pursued in a social context, such as a school, there are often side issues which come to bear. Janet Waters' view was particularly important because she and her husband were becoming very influential in the Tordale school community. They represent the middle-class core of the Blockies and are typical of the Blockies' abilities to organise and agitate for their own ends. The tension between the Blockies and the Farmers was aggravated by issues such as health and human relationships teaching at the school. For the Blockies, whose interests also extended to peace studies and improving the performing and creative arts teaching at the school, the Farmers were under-educated conservatives. For the Farmers, who were mainly interested in leaving the teaching to the teachers, but whose curricular interests were more concerned with the '3-Rs', the Blockies were noisy 'trendies'.

The initiative for the health and human relationships curriculum came from the mothers' club. The concerns of the Blockies were articulated in terms which incorporated the Farmers. Emphasis was placed upon traditional, gender segregated notions of respect for boys and girls. The 'ladies-first' form of chivalry was espoused alongside fears over the approaching adolescent sexuality of the sixth grade children. At the October meeting of the mothers' club, which was usually held a day or two before the council meeting, it was decided to raise the matter at the council meeting through the mothers' club's representative. However, at this stage the mothers had not clearly defined their aims or strategy. Their intention was to raise the issue and argue for an improved course at the school and for a meeting to be held by the school council, at which 'experts' would help inform parents about such matters.

Karen Hersch, the mother's club representative, raised the matter of the health and human relationships curriculum during her report to the school council. Usually the mothers' club report is received with little discussion. Karen Hersch said that the children didn't enjoy the present health and human relationships curriculum because it was largely irrelevant to them. The principal was visibly irritated, but said nothing, probably because Karen Hersch moved immediately to the next item of her report about inter-school sports.

This item prompted some discussion and the health and human relationships issue was forgotten.

Later in the meeting the principal, in his own report to council, inserted a comment about 'sex education' at the school. Rod Miles endeavoured to accommodate some of the mothers' clubs' concerns within an *agenda* he constructed around the issues. He recounted an event from that day involving a grade six girl fainting with stomach cramps and the other children 'panicking and being silly'. Other council members joined the discussion, which included some light-hearted banter from the men at the principal's expense. Karen Hersch took this opportunity to explain the mother's club's views in more detail. The men on the council, apart from John Sheriff, were Farmers and they shrank from discussing the intimate matters which Karen Hersch was placing on her *agenda*. Rod Miles was not to be deterred; he actively debated the issues with the women on the school council. A vital point of conflict occurred over the matter of a public meeting. The women argued for a parents' meeting attended by some 'experts' to explain both the medical-biological matters and the shape that a new health and human relationships curriculum should take. The women had their 'experts' in mind, one of whom was known to Rod Miles as a 'radical' sex educator from a nearby secondary school. He opposed the idea and recommended that the council refrain from such involvement. However, he agreed that there was nothing to stop the parents arranging a meeting themselves. Eventually, the council decided not to proceed with the matter, but said that it had no objection to a group of parents organising a meeting.

The interested parents, principally Blockie mothers, organised the meeting for an evening in November. They received little cooperation from Rod Miles who was organising the teachers according to his own *agenda*. Fifteen parents attended for what was an open discussion of matters concerned with adolescent sexuality and health and human relationships teaching. None of the school staff attended the meeting: something which was interpreted negatively by the parents concerned.

In his report to the December mothers' club meeting the principal mentioned the new courses for the following year at the school. He discussed the outline of the new health and human relationships curriculum which, he noted, conformed to Education Department guidelines. Rod Miles and Donna Morton would teach health and human relationships to the grade five and six children. Janet Waters stated that there appeared to be little new in the course and asked the principal to distribute some related booklets she had obtained to the staff and other parents. The principal became annoyed and said,

'There never has been, or never will be, by the school council or the mothers' club an ability to order what the teachers do or do not teach.'

He then talked of 'a process of consensus' between the teachers and the parents being required. However, his emphasis on adhering to the Education Department's guidelines proved to be a clinching argument. The mothers' club did not raise the issue at the council meeting two days later.

Janet Waters circulated the booklets amongst the staff and some parents. The teachers were unanimously opposed to this intrusion. Donna Morton said that although she welcomed parental involvement in the school, this time 'they had overstepped the mark—a line has to be drawn somewhere.' Stephanie Bell said that she felt strongly about the issue: 'A booklet came around and they (the parents) wanted the teachers to deal with the things in it. I felt that they weren't the sort of things to teach children'.

The issue petered out, never to be raised again. However, some of the side-issues riding with the health and human relationships issue took on lives of their own. Nutrition became a source of dispute in 1984 and divided the mothers' club. The Farmer mothers said that their Blockie counterparts were implying that they 'were neglectful of their children's welfare'. As we have already seen, the Blockies had taken control of the new, more powerful, 1984 school council and now the Farmers began to resist the rise of the Blockie *agenda* in the community. During 1985, parents' concerns about a lack of lunchtime supervision and discipline reached a head. The Blockies pressed the issue, but the Farmers concurred. A Blockie mother presented a letter of complaint, essentially about the principal, to a school council meeting with a request that it be distributed to all parents. The president of the school council advised the council members that they could face legal action if the letter was distributed. The matter rested there. The author of the letter removed her children from the school.

Some reflections on the Tordale case studies

Clearly, the two issues in the case studies are quite different, as are the outcomes. The *agendas* surrounding these two issues are areas of contestation, continuously being manipulated, shaped, defended or attacked by the people involved. However, the interests and motivations of the participants are not clearcut. Teachers' and Blockies' values are rooted in the middle class, but they are divided along teacher-parent lines. Gender relationships help cement the principal and Blockie men together and separate them from the women. Little seems to join the women teachers and the Blockie women together. The Farmers are linked by their labour, even if their class positions vary between landowners and labourers. On occasions, gender relationships bond the Farmer and Blockie mothers together, but on others they are at loggerheads.

The power to control the *agendas* surrounding one's life is a product of social position, personality and knowledge. The two most powerful people in the case studies, and in the school in general, are the principal and the president. The position of principal is a senior appointment in an education system, with specific responsibilities and powers over the lives of adults and children in schools. A stream of information from the educational bureaucracy and from local networks flows to the principal. In contrast, the president occupies a voluntary, spare-time position and relies heavily on the principal for information. Most principals possess a substantial accumulation of knowledge about the operation of schooling throughout their careers as teachers, deputy principals etc. In a small school, such as Tordale, the most senior teacher in the school is appointed as the head teacher, because the school's size does not warrant a principal. However, head teachers are usually called principals in their communities and, especially if men, attract commensurate power and authority.

In the two case studies, people other than the principal set the *agenda* for the council and, more particularly in the case of the health and human relationships issue, for the school at large. The mower issue was instigated by the second most powerful person in the school community, John Sheriff. He used his position and knowledge to influence the outcome of events. As president, he was able to introduce the topic of the ride-on mower into discussion at three consecutive meetings. His knowledge of the people, and his presiding at the meetings, meant that he could maximise his chances of receiving a good hearing. He developed his knowledge of the ride-on mowers to the extent that he was seen by council members as an authority on the subject. *A gender agenda* exists: mowing is an activity which is articulated and debated by men on the council. John Sheriff's language, replete with mechanical terms, established his expertise with the men and relegated the women to bystanders in a debate which was fundamentally about spending the money they raised.

Some women, mostly Blockies, resented John Sheriff's methods as president and others, mostly Farmers, held him in high esteem. For example, one Farmer mother observed, 'he is just great with ideas and going for them'. Another saw the president as being occasionally indifferent to other council members, especially women: 'If he knows about it (an item of discussion) anyway he mightn't listen quite as much to you, but if he's not sure he will.'

Karen Hersch, a Blockie mother and instigator of the fun run, was even more pointed. She said, 'I feel personally put down as a women (by the president)'. The president's dealings were seen, by women like Karen Hersch, as part of a strategy to ensure success for his ideas and failure for theirs. Women had no influence over the outcome of the mower case; the Farmers saw this as men's business and the Blockies knew they would not be taken seriously.

The mower case represented a powerful man's single-handed attempt to achieve something in his own interests as president of the school council and as the person responsible for organising the grass-cutting. There was no opposition to John Sheriff's proposal in principle, but there was some questioning by the fathers of the various machines' capabilities, and from the principal about the financial arrangements. Had either of these two sections of the council opposed the mower, it would have been interesting to speculate on the way the women would have argued and voted. Probably, the principal was the only one who could have stopped it, because the fathers, being so few in number, could easily be outvoted. The principal's opinions were respected by some of the mothers and by the fathers, therefore, he could be expected to have influenced enough votes to defeat the president.

The case of the health and human relationships curriculum shows a group of women, mostly Blockies, shaping the *agenda*. However, their power in the community was circumscribed, particularly by the principal and teachers. They set the *agenda* for the mothers' clubs' thinking, debate and action; they influenced the broader community thinking; but they could not, through the school council, set the *agenda* for the school. In effect, the principal excluded the women's *agenda* from the school. This circumscription was so tight that, even though many hours of discussion and action were expended on this issue by women in the community, only seven minutes were given to it at the school council. In contrast, the mower issue took over an hour across three council meetings, and involved no community debate.

The Blockie mothers pressing the issue made some tactical errors which galvanised the principal and teachers into direct opposition. Their emphasis on the use of 'experts' made the teachers and principal feel particularly threatened. They also made some of the Farmer mothers and fathers feel uncomfortable about the range of sexuality and contraception matters covered in distributed booklets and public discussion. The principal, in this respect, probably knew these parents better than did the Blockies. He saw himself as a mediator between the Blockies and Farmers and had learnt a good deal about their separate values and interests. As the school is the community focal point, it forms a venue where Blockie–Farmer conflicts can be mediated or exacerbated. Therefore, the principal was able to keep the health and human relationships issue controlled by selectively seeding the minds, and fuelling the concerns, of some of the Farmers. He knew that the Farmers—whose lives, ironically, often revolve around animal reproduction processes—were the most jittery about the teaching of human sexuality and reproduction processes to their children.

For the health and human relationships issue to succeed the school council or the school staff would have had to take action on the matter. If the president had been in favour then the school council debate would have been more substantial. This could have led to a parent-teacher meeting and the development of a health and human relationships curriculum policy. However, prevailing gender relationships leave matters of health and human relationships to women, which would have discouraged John Sheriff from being involved. Even if the school council had decided to develop a health and human relationships policy for the school it would have required the support of the staff to be effected. The main reason, as Rod Miles knew only too well, was that the 1983 school council did not have the power to enforce such policy decisions or to directly control the school's curriculum. One year later and things would have been different. By 1984 the school council had more power over the curriculum—and it was controlled by Blockies.

Linfield and the special development school

In this case study the initiative for the issue pursued by Linfield primary school council came as the result of a directive from the Regional Director of Education. The directive, which coincided with the commencement of our research at the school, required that Linfield school re-establish a planning committee to prepare for the relocation of the local Special Developmental School (SDS) on the Linfield school site. A little history is useful here.

The SDS is set on a leased site about two kilometres from Linfield primary school. It is staffed by women, most of whom are high on dedication and low on qualifications. Throughout its 25 years, this organisation has provided care and education for local intellectually disabled children. The SDS has a reputation for pioneering teaching programmes for intellectually disabled children, for example in reading skills. Ironically, the success of people such as the SDS women increases their vulnerability. As they show that intellectually disabled children can learn and benefit from education, then the emphasis shifts from providing day care to schooling. In recent years, such places have become 'schools' in the present Ministry of Education, instead of day training centres under the old Mental Retardation Division of the Health Department. Once in the grip of the education bureaucracy, the role, classification and qualifications of SDS 'teachers' came under scrutiny. The Victorian Teachers' Union also cast its eye in their direction.

In the early 1980s, the Education Department adopted a 'normalisation' or 'mainstreaming' policy to integrate disabled children, where possible, into 'normal' schools. At this time, Linfield primary school was linked with the SDS by the Education Department for the purpose of implementing the new policy. The popular belief was that the reason these two schools were linked was because Linfield had the largest primary school site in the town. When the Labor government came to power in 1982, a two year pause took place while their own policy was developed (Report of the Ministerial Review of Educational Services for the Integration of the Disabled, 1984). This pause coincided with a reorganisation of the Education Department and meant that Linfield and the SDS largely forgot the matter.

The issue was resurrected in 1983 when it was known that the lease for the SDS site would not be renewed on its expiry in 1984. The regional office of the Education Department was attempting to solve the problem by relocating the SDS on the Linfield school site. A planning committee was formed and, in line with government policing for community participation, it comprised staff and parents from both schools and was chaired by the local Senior Education Officer (SEO). Due to the likely significance of this issue to the research project, permission was sought to attend planning committee meetings and to interview those involved.

At both schools there existed a resigned reluctance towards the relocation. However, at Linfield there were several staff, including Ted Symes, who were responsive to new developments in education. They influenced the school to set about its task with a willingness which belied the initial reluctance. The council selected Brian Garden, the president, and Andrew Masters, who was eventually to become the president of the new council, as the parent representatives. Miriam Tate, a staff representative on council, was selected as the teacher representative. Hence, including the principal, the four Linfield members of the planning committee were council members. This was probably inevitable, given the lack of parent participation in the school. However, these male parents were chosen for their perceived ability to cope with the anticipated hard negotiations over the issue.

'Tough decisions' and 'hard fights' were expected and, thus, a masculine *agenda* was being constructed.

The only female parent on the school council, Jane Peters, the parents' club representative, was a reluctant contributor at school council meetings. She was regarded as hesitant and, thus, not a contender for a place on a planning committee with such a masculine *agenda*. Ironically, the men experienced problems arranging their work in order to attend planning committee meetings, which Jane Peters, who had been, in her words, 'just a mother for the last six years' would not have done. Steve Weston, who, along with Miriam Tate, was a regular staff representative at the council meetings, was a gentle and sensitive person, who appeared to other council members to possess less of the 'masculine' qualities of 'tough talking' than Miriam Tate.

Several people, especially the principal, began to study what was involved in 'mainstreaming' and SDS relocation from other schools which had implemented such developments. They visited the SDS to see it at work and to talk to the principal, staff and parents; good will was soon established. Both schools had reservations about the relocation, but Linfield people thought the problems could be solved. Gradually, several of the influential staff at Linfield became convinced that 'mainstreaming' was good for all children. This represented a significant development, because it meant that Linfield was willing to proceed with the relocation and with some measure of integration. Such a willingness was neatly within Education Department policy, but it caused alarm at the SDS. They saw their school being swamped by the much larger Linfield school. The SDS staff also had concerns about the Education Department's and the Victorian Teachers' Union's likely stances on their qualifications and admission to the Primary Teachers' Classified Roll. The all female staff at the SDS felt in danger of being subsumed within the (male dominated) organisation at Linfield or within an unknown, future organisation at the school when the present staff had left.

Linfield school arranged for a group of staff and parents including Andrew Masters, Miriam Tate and Jane Peters from the council, to take a day and half visit to another school where a similar relocation had taken place. This visit, in October 1983, marked a watershed in Linfield's understanding. By all accounts, the school they visited was a battleground of acrimony and antagonism between the antecedent institutions. In the opinion of the Linfield people, this severely detracted from the children's schooling and the working lives of the staff. Reports were given to a Linfield staff meeting attended by the SEO chairing the planning committee. Some staff, especially the all-male senior staff, began calling for written and explicit agreements between the schools on administration, staffing, resources etc., before proceeding further. Ted Symes and Miriam Tate tried to moderate these demands by pointing to the current good relationships between the schools. However, the deputy principal, James Porter, who was probably the most influential person in the school, insisted that it was unworkable to have two principals of one school and, thus, all the proposed administrative and organisational changes had to be agreed in advance. Clearly, the Linfield staff were debating the integration of the two schools and not just the SDS relocation.

By now the concerns of the SDS were becoming reality as the Linfield school began to use its power to ensure its interests were served in any new amalgamated structure. Recognising the contentious nature of the issue, the SEO assured the staff that, 'no decision will be made without consultation' and that, 'the situation is very fluid'. The *agenda* became firmly masculine as the men took their positions to debate power and resources, not educational principles, children's lives or the livelihoods of the SDS staff.

At the council meeting six days later, Miriam Tate attempted to shift the *agenda* to matters of principle and people. She said it was important for the staff and community to understand the principles of the integration of children with disabilities into 'mainstream' schooling, and she recommended the school undertake to explain these principles to parents. She also raised the matter of staffing and the 'tagging' of positions in relation to the teaching of the intellectually disabled. The principal raised the matter of the qualifications of the staff at the SDS. He believed that the Education Department would allow people until 1987 to improve their qualifications to the minimum required for primary school teaching. There was some discussion of the implications of this for the SDS staff, during which the principal said that he believed 'they would be O.K.' However, Hilda Stone, who was representing the parents' club because Jane Peters could not attend, said she believed that at least two of the SDS staff would have difficulties because of their lack of formal teaching qualifications. Her understanding was to prove to be the most accurate of any council member's expressed at the time.

Prue Cameron, the SDS principal, confirmed that the problems over teaching qualifications would affect nearly all SDS staff. She reflected ruefully that even though she was a BA graduate and had worked at the SDS or its antecedents for 23 years, mostly as principal or equivalent, she might become a teacher-aide in any integration. One cannot underestimate the deep personal worries someone like Prue Cameron faces with such a prospect. The men of Linfield had no idea, although some of the women knew. The danger was not merely one of loss of status and job satisfaction, and of being forced to add study to a busy woman's life. It was the disintegration of a small, close-knit, caring community for intellectually disabled children. A community which was established through a 25 year struggle against the massed ranks of professionals, bureaucrats and prejudiced public.

* * *

A week after the October Linfield council meeting, the SDS arranged for the school council to meet the SDS staff and management committee. Ted Symes opened the discussion and it was soon clear that the visit to an 'integrated' school and the subsequent meetings at Linfield school had added some circumspection to his approach. He raised several problems to do with the administration of the 'integration' of the two schools. His choice of the term 'integration', instead of 'relocation', was to prove significant. The SDS raised several questions concerning the operation of the two schools. It was stated by the SDS that although there could be a shared administration block, 'to help overcome any personality problems and communication breakdowns,' there needed to be two separate schools, 'because the needs of the children are different'. It was argued by Linfield school that a single school council was necessary, which the SDS questioned on the grounds that there might be insufficient recognition of their children's special needs in the allocation of resources and equipment. The SDS people were surprised at the commitment that Linfield was applying to fulfilling the Regional Office's relocation directive. The SDS expected a good deal of reluctance from Linfield, but were witnessing relatively speedy progress on their part. This, and the fact that integration was now on the *agenda*, prompted the SDS to give much more serious attention to the issue. They began to fight the issue on the basis of the *agenda* which had been set by Linfield.

A week after the meeting with the SDS, the Linfield school council held an extraordinary meeting devoted to the SDS issue. The SEO attended the meeting. The president asked for reports on the meeting with the SDS and the visit to the 'integrated' school. These were led or presented by male council members. Miriam Tate, who had visited the 'integrated' school, and Jane Peters, who attended both visits—the latter had also been to the SDS meeting—said nothing at this stage. The president did not ask for their thoughts and they did not assert them. In addition, Miriam Tate, as at previous meetings, was asked by the president to record the minutes. She always resisted such requests, partly because she felt she was being asked because she was a woman, however, with the SEO present, acceded in spite of her visible reluctance. This restricted her opportunity to contribute, because she was concentrating on recording others' comments.

Ted Symes helped to formalise a shift in the *agenda* by talking of the 'integration' as amounting to a shared administration 'block' (i.e. a building), 'preferably housing all staff with intermingling as much as possible'. The 'normalisation' or 'mainstreaming' policy which underpinned integration was now problematic for the two schools. Prue Cameron had said that the 'philosophy is fine, the practicalities are a concern'; now Ted Symes was following suit.

The council meeting was dominated for the first 45 minutes by three men: the president, the principal and Andrew Masters. Later, the matter of the two principals was raised and the SEO entered the debate. He said that the principal of Linfield school was 'an A-grade (the most senior grade) principal and more senior than the principal of the SDS'. The council discussion, substantially maintained by these four men, then centred on the notion of a single hierarchy with a 'super principal' or 'el supremo' at the top.

Then the question of resources for the new school was raised. The president and Andrew Masters endeavoured to haggle with the regional office, through the SEO, in order to obtain the 'cyclic' maintenance work for the school in exchange for the council's compliance with the proposed relocation of the SDS. 'Cyclic' maintenance was an issue at the school because, due to government spending cuts, this periodic maintenance of school buildings had been deferred and the condition of the school was deteriorating. The SEO dispelled quickly any ideas of such a deal, however, he assured them that, 'there should be no diminution of the resources available to this school'. Andrew Masters, the main haggler, said: 'We do not want to see the Education Department maintain the SDS in pristine condition when doing this place (Linfield) in the eye...it is necessary to bring the school up to a reasonable standard'. He later stated to the SEO: 'Before we go in we want to know what the Education Department is going to put into it.' To which the SEO replied, 'If you want to win races you've got to realise that you are not going to get cyclic maintenance just because you are being integrated with a SDS.'

The SEO later suggested that the new SDS building may have 'a low maintenance requirement' so that 'maintenance money may be directed' to the primary school. It was interpreted that a new administration block for both schools would be a physical gain in space for Linfield, because it would enable the existing administration areas to be used in other ways. The SEO offered a thinly veiled inducement to the staff by suggesting that the new administration building might include a new staffroom. Apart from one contribution, the whole of this debate about resources, which lasted for forty minutes, was conducted by four men: the president, principal, SEO and Andrew Masters.

The meeting continued for another two hours, dominated by the same four men. Towards the end of the meeting there was considerable debate about the power of the school council to veto the relocation and to refuse to join the planning committee. In essence they were demonstrating the tension between different government policies. In this case, between a policy leading to greater autonomy for local school councils, and another concerned with integrating disabled children into the 'mainstream' of schooling.

The SEO produced a motion, prepared prior to the meeting, which expressed the council's compliance with the regional director's directive to relocate the SDS at Linfield and which also requested the regional director to form a planning committee for the new school 'with appropriate administrative support'. The president objected to the unquestioning compliance of the motion. After some discussion it was agreed to add the words, 'to consider all matters pertaining (to the relocation of the SDS at Linfield)' to the motion requesting a formal planning committee be established by the Regional Director. The amendment would invite the planning committee to consider the broader administrative and educational aspects of the relocation, together with the usual matters of buildings and grounds. The debate over the wording of the motion took 44 minutes after which the president observed: 'The three people who have discussed this motion are the three people who have no right to do so.' What he meant was not that they could not discuss the motion, but that the three men who dominated the discussion: the president, the principal and the SEO, could not propose or second a motion at a council meeting. It was necessary to find council members to do this. At first no one would volunteer to propose the motion. Then Steve Weston offered, but a seconder proved even harder to find. It was only after the president said that the motion would lapse if it was not seconded, that Miriam Tate agreed to second the motion. She was later to say in an interview that the only reason she did this was to curtail the meeting.

The time was 10.15 pm, many people were tired and keen to leave. The membership and composition of the planning committee was covered before the meeting finished at 11.00 pm. The preceding three and a half hours were crucial to the formulation of the council's policy and procedures concerning the relocation of the SDS. The meeting was dominated by four men and at no stage was Jane Peters involved, even though she was one of three people present who had attended both visits. Gender was powerfully shaping the *agenda*.

Three weeks later, in December 1983, at the first meeting of the planning committee, chaired by the SEO, it was emphasised by both schools that they had not agreed to the relocation, but were merely considering it. The meeting aired many of the schools' concerns and they wanted further consideration of what was at stake. The SDS was keen to discuss the matter with all their parents and staff, which could not be done until the new school year.

* * *

The matter proceeded no further. A meeting attended by 38 parents and ten staff at the SDS was held in February 1984. The discussion ranged over the eight or so points that the meeting felt were likely to affect deleteriously the education of the SDS children if the relocation, and possible integration, went ahead. The following motion was passed unanimously: 'That the community of the Special Developmental School expresses the wish that the school remain on its present site and the buildings be extensively renovated.'

It emerged that the lease, after all, could be renewed on the SDS site. Prue Cameron immediately began wresting from the regional office some of the half a million dollars that had been allocated to the SDS relocation, for the renovation of the existing buildings. Linfield school took no further part in the proceedings.

Reflections on the Linfield case

This third case study is a larger and more complicated affair than the previous two at Tordale. Its direct origins were outside the school in the regional office of the Education Department and its dealings included another party in the form of the SDS. In a more indirect, but nevertheless powerful, sense this issue had its origins within government policies about the integration of disabled people into the community at large, and the education system, in particular. Hence the *agenda* shaping processes within the council were partly in response to the actions of outside parties, in particular, the SDS.

Perhaps the main practical reason why the *agenda* for the debate about the relocation of the SDS at Linfield was shaped by men is that they occupied the key positions. As at Tordale, both the president and the principal were men, as were the future president—Andrew Masters, the deputy principal—James Porter, all the senior teachers in the school and the union branch president. The teachers are considered in the next chapter, but, in terms of the effect upon the school council debate, and the broader *agenda* for the issue's debate within the school, it can be seen that nowhere is there a significant powerful feminine contribution. Nowhere, that is, until one looks beyond Linfield to the SDS, which was entirely staffed by women.

The proof of the shallowness of popular support for the powerful Linfield council men, and the SEO, came at the final meeting, when there was considerable difficulty in obtaining support for the SEO-initiated motion. This was because the men's *agenda* did not include the practical and personal implications of integrating the children, which the other council members knew affected both the parents', and the staff's, acceptance of the matter. The *agenda* was shaped progressively by the men as their knowledge and experience of what was at stake increased. Initially, the principal moved the *agenda* to be about integration, rather than relocation. The visit to the 'integrated' school was an important knowledge-gathering experience which shifted the *agenda* from integration to the pursuit of a single administration and principal. The visit to the local SDS, where women began to affect the outcome, saw the *agenda* shift again to one of buildings and resources. The shallowness of this final position, which was reduced simply to a Linfield-centred greed over money, would have been a difficult one upon which to found a successful relocation of the SDS, let alone any integration of the education of the children at the schools.

In the end the SDS women won. However, their win was only in the context of the SDS itself, the broader issues of Government and Education Department policies about normalisation and integration were unaffected. The matter of their qualifications and status as teachers within the Education Department remained problematic. This caused some friction between the teachers at the SDS and the Victorian Teachers' Union, of which they were members.

Concluding comment

School councils are used as a conduit for the state to structure the educational practice of schools. However, as the Linfield case study shows, school councils do have the capacity to move beyond this limited function. Had the SDS issue been resolved in line with the original directive then, presumably, the work practices and lives of both adults and children involved would have been substantially different. Some council members, especially men, and in particular those who occupy powerful council positions, are able to shape council policy and action in their own interests. Or, as in the case of the health and human relationships curriculum issue at Tordale, to resist others' attempts to do likewise. Giddens has discussed the ways in which people as 'purposive agents' are able to 'act-back' (dialectically) on the organisations and structures of which they are members (1979:114, 1984:2-7). He argues that, as a result of 'reflexive knowledgeability' people are able to evaluate rationally their practice and to plan their actions accordingly. This leads to a continuity of practice which is embedded within, and yet 'acts-back' upon, the social structure. In this sense, we can see the Linfield and Tordale school council members calculating their actions from their knowledge of the school community and of wider matters which they can bring to bear on the council.

School councils and all such organisations are locations of discourse between people with a mixture of competing and complementary interests. The competition may be obvious, such as that between teachers and parents, or it may emanate from more general conflicts, such as those between the Tordale Blockies and Farmers, or from individual interests, such as those of Deidre Best and Jane Waters. Complementary interests may be within groups of the council, such as the Tordale Blockie or Farmer groups, or across broader social divisions, such as those to do with gender. The whole council may also be seen to have complementary interests as, for example, when Linfield council members began to act in concert in relation to the SDS or the regional office.

The Linfield and Tordale school councils used *agendas* to structure their discourse. These *agendas* represent the boundaries of knowledge and values which are allowed into the discourse. They are formed by people: perhaps by the principal in response to his interests or responsibilities, or perhaps by agencies outside of the school, such as the regional educational bureaucracy. People, especially the men who occupied powerful positions on the councils, were able to change the *agendas* used in council discourse. Some of these changes gave prominence to what might be called 'masculine' properties of discourse, hence suppressing 'feminine' concerns, and diminishing participation by women.

The school councils did not allow equal participation by all members of their communities in forming and debating the *agendas*. At Tordale, the middle-class drive toward matters educational, administrative and bureaucratic was largely enacted by women. Middle-class values about what constituted a 'good' diet, a 'good' education and even a 'good' mother were, on some occasions, translated across class divisions and, on others, exacerbated them. The annual fun run exemplifies the former; the dispute over saveloys exemplifies the latter. The Government's consensus politics, which drives its policies on community participation in school councils, is based on the middle-class premise that consensuses are reached at school council meetings by the representation and discussion of the issues which are constructed in schools' *agendas*. It ignores the factors—such as gender, class and ethnicity—which contribute to differences in people's powers to shape *agendas* and discourse. It also fails to recognise that the school council itself emerges out of middle-class politics as the peak form of community participation in schooling.

Tordale and Linfield councils show that in working-class communities, such as Linfield, the level of parental participation on school councils is minute and dominated by a few middle-class men. And in communities with a substantial middle-class component, such as Tordale, the participation may be higher, but will continue to reflect the same pattern of domination. Chapter 5 presents the nature and composition of the Linfield and Tordale school communities in more detail and the parents' views about education, the schools and their communities are discussed. In the next chapter teachers, the other people in the adults' school world, are the focus.

4 The teachers

I was taken by Miriam Tate's biography. It reflects many of the themes emerging in this book: the strength of gender in shaping family and educational experiences; the power of individuals to construct their own agendas; *the links between generation and gender; and the contradictions that emerge when gender relationships are intertwined with other social divisions. I have recounted a brief biography of her life here from my discussions with her. Other elements of her life surface throughout the book.*

Brought up on a Mallee farm in the 1940s, Miriam Tate experienced the tensions and contradictions that litter the histories of rural, working-class families. Her maternal grandmother was 'quite a strong feminist' and raised her mother to be a determined and independent woman. Just before World War II, Miriam Tate's mother was a technician in the emerging photographic industry in Melbourne; later, marriage took her away to an alien farming life on the vast plains of north-western Victoria. In contrast, Miriam Tate saw her paternal grandmother as believing that the 'rights should go to boys, and girls marry for boys to look after them'. Her paternal grandmother had eight children and ruled domestic life in the home while her husband worked the farm. Miriam Tate's grandmothers brought their contradictory influences to bear during her childhood, directly, through her immediate experience of these women and also indirectly through the lives of their children—her parents, aunts and uncles—as she grew up amongst them.

At age six, Miriam Tate attended her first school. The nearest school to the family farm was ten kilometres away which, on the rough unmade roads of the time, was a formidable distance. So, for the first two years of her schooling, she boarded with an aunt some twenty kilometres away. Even this arrangement left her with a five kilometre walk to and from school each day. She returned home at weekends and holidays, but she deeply resented her frequent absences from the family. Her younger brother was the butt of her resentment and received regular thumpings when his sister was home. Eventually, when she was eight years old her parents succumbed to her requests to stay at home. Her brother was about to start school and it would have been difficult for the parents to have boarded out both children. So, it was decided that correspondence school would serve to provide the children's education.

Miriam Tate recalls that her mother 'nearly went mad' over the following two years trying to tutor her two children, who were much more interested in playing around the farm than schooling. Her father decided he would buy two horses so that they could ride the ten kilometres to school. This proved to be a disaster. The horses were two 'scruffy brumbies', who spent more time throwing Miriam and her brother into ditches, than transporting them to and from school. With a catastrophe appearing imminent, her father jettisoned the equine transport in favour of bicycles. The roads had improved: from very rough, unformed ones to rough formed ones! Given sufficient skill, the journey could be cycled without falling off. The bikes also had the big advantage of not bolting off over the far horizon and leaving their riders stranded!

After primary school, Miriam Tate's secondary schooling was at home by correspondence. This time, it was her brother who left home for a boarding school. Miriam Tate began to feel the yoke of gender more heavily than ever before. She had to end her correspondence schooling after three years and run the family dairy herd. Her father decided to keep his son at boarding school and stop his daughter's schooling. Miriam Tate's mother was strongly opposed to this decision, 'but in farming communities it's the farmers who come first over their wives'. Her father accepted his own mother's view of the place of women in the world. Money was said to be the reason, but Miriam and her mother were 'kept in the dark about the amount of money we really had'. Later, after Miriam had married, the family farm was to run into financial difficulties, brought about by several years of poor rainfall and drought. Her father was about to sell-up and leave, but her mother refused and insisted they should stick the hard times out. This they did and, largely due to her mother's persistence, the farm survived and turned into a source of significant family wealth.

Miriam married a primary school teacher and built her life around his career and their forthcoming family. Her first teaching experience came at this time when she was employed as a 'sewing mistress' at her husband's small rural school. In effect, she became an untrained teacher of the youngest children in the school. She worked for a year and, she said, with 'a lot of help from my husband', it proved to be an enjoyable and formative experience. The Education Department's district inspector reported favourably on her work and recommended she train as a teacher. However, with a young daughter in a relatively isolated, rural community, it was impossible to study.

Miriam Tate's husband was promoted to another school several hundred kilometres away in eastern Victoria. She gave birth to a son and had a variety of temporary jobs during the ensuing years. She 'always took jobs so that I could be home when they (the children) came home from school'. She became friends with a woman and they talked about their interests in pursuing tertiary study. A process of mutual support and encouragement led them to enrol in different institutions and help each other through their first two years. Miriam Tate enrolled in a teacher education course at a local college and immediately encountered problems within her family. Her daughter, who was in her final year at high school, encouraged her mother to study, but her son, who had just started his secondary education, was resentful. Her husband, who was also studying part-time to improve his qualifications, actively supported her studies. Because she felt obliged to be available for her children, Miriam Tate started her evening studies at 10 pm when they slept. She became exhausted, especially during practice teaching.

The males in Miriam Tate's life, rather like her parents and grandparents before them, reacted in powerfully different ways to her being a student. Her husband provided her with support, encouragement and often practical assistance. Her son gradually increased his resistance to her study to the extent of self-inflicted deterioration in his own education. To his parents' distress he left school early to take an apprenticeship as a machine-fitter: something they thought ill-suited him. He was a source of worry and guilt to her. She had 'thought that when I [went] teaching I [would] put him through university', but her desire to give him the education she was denied was foiled by his attempts to force her back into her home. Her daughter followed the family line from Miriam Tate's maternal grandmother and emerged as a determined and independent woman. She completed her Higher School Certificate and pursued a successful career.

Miriam Tate qualified as a teacher at the end of 1979. Her career began in a manner common to other contemporary primary teaching graduates. She had a one year drift from unemployment, through emergency teaching at different schools, to a teaching position. In 1981, she accepted a job at Linfield primary school. At first she worked as a teacher-librarian and as a support teacher. She spent two years teaching grade three classes and then, at her request, she moved to take a preparatory (universally known as 'prep') grade. This was one of the classes I observed for a week during early 1983. She was, as we have seen in the previous chapter, a school council member.

The girl who completed the minimum schooling, most of it by correspondence on the family's Mallee farm, had worked her way to spending the latter part of her working life in a classroom.

Gender and primary teaching

When Miriam Tate became a Victorian primary school teacher in 1980 she joined about 25 000 others. The Ministry of Education in Victoria consumes around one per cent of Australia's Gross National Product and employs, across all staff, about one per cent of the Australian workforce (Frazer, Dunstan and Creed, 1985: vii). If all things were equal between the sexes, then one half the employees would be women and the distribution through all levels and types of positions should be similarly equal. However, primary school teaching is 'dominated' by women. In 1984, 72 per cent of primary school teachers were women. This evident inequality might suggest an affirmative action policy for men, but closer scrutiny of the distribution of men and women throughout primary teaching, and the Ministry of Education itself, shows that it is men who hold the positions of power.

Table 4.1 shows the numbers and percentages of men and women teachers in Victorian schools during our research in 1984. In Victoria, teachers who are employed continuously are appointed as 'temporary' teachers and then allocated to a school. Temporary teachers may apply to become 'classified' teachers, which means that they are placed on the classified roll of 'permanent' teachers according to their qualifications and experience. Classified teachers are required to join the State superannuation scheme and are eligible to apply for promotion. Generally, promotion is gained on the basis of a teacher's seniority in years of service. However, this simple picture is complicated by other procedures which have applied in the past, such as minimum qualification levels for types of promotion, inspector's reports, principal's recommendations, different rolls for men and women, and promotion quotas for men and women. Typically, it takes twenty or more years of teaching to achieve promotion from Band One to Principal. This usually means at least four promotions, each of which often involves a change of schools and homes.

Table 4.1 shows a gradual shedding of female representation as

Table 4.1 Distribution of men and women primary schoolteachers in Victoria by seniority, March 1984.

Seniority level	male	female	% female	Total
Principal (Grade A & B)	726	150	19	876
Band 4	592	117	17	709
Band 3	972	636	40	1608
(head teacher)	211	26	11	237
Band 2	1394	2808	67	4202
(head teacher)	358	107	23	465
Band 1	2257	12215	84	14472
(head teacher)	117	130	53	247
Temporary teachers	231	1621	88	1852
Total	6976	17851	72	24827

Source: Compiled from: Education Dept. of Victoria, Policy and Planning Unit, 1984.

seniority increases. In small schools, such as Tordale, the 'principal' is actually a teacher designated as head teacher who fulfils the administrative responsibilities of a principal, in terms of organising school council elections, maintaining rolls, ordering materials and so forth. In small communities this vests a head teacher, such as Rod Miles, with the name, status and influence commensurate with that of a real principal, such as Ted Symes. Rod Miles and James Porter, a deputy principal at Linfield who had spent nine years as a head teacher in a small rural school, both said that they relished the opportunity to be, in Porter's words, 'your own boss'. None of the women in our study had been 'head teachers'. This accords with the even lower percentages of women head teachers in comparison with the proportions of women in the equivalent band level in Table 4.1.

As approximately 70 per cent of primary teachers are women, one might expect the same proportions at each level in the teaching employment structure. However, only about 20 per cent of principals are women. Obviously, especially given the way power is distributed in relation to seniority, it is men who dominate primary schools both in Australia (Sampson, 1986a) and internationally (Lacey, 1977:31-35). In 1977, the Victorian Committee on Equal Opportunity in Schools concluded that, 'It is thus clear that men alone are making the all important administrative decisions about the education of boys and girls in Victoria, including those which govern the regulations on which teacher promotions are based' (1977:101). The committee was concerned at the lack of women in senior positions, not only in schools, but also in the educational bureaucracy.

In the seven years between the publication of the report and our research, as was discussed in previous chapters, the administration of education in Victoria has been through a sequence of sweeping changes. These changes did not bring forth more women into the top echelons of the educational bureaucracy in Victoria. In 1984, the top 31 positions in the Education Department, from the director-general to the regional directors, were entirely occupied by men. The most senior women were to be found as deputy regional directors, where they comprised 17 per cent of the total (Education Department of Victoria, Policy and Planning Unit, 1984:25).

The position in the primary school teachers' union, the VTU, reflects a similar, if less extreme, imbalance. In June 1985, men comprised nearly two-thirds of the appointed officers, elected officers and state council members of the VTU. This pattern is repeated in the Australian Teachers' Federation (ATF), which is the national organisation of teacher unions (Foggo, 1986:4-6). Over the past decade there have been many efforts throughout the ATF's affiliates to increase the representation of women in their peak decision-making and administrative bodies. Indeed, the South Australian Institute of Teachers (SAIT) requires that there be an equal representation of the sexes on its executive and standing committees. However, as Foggo has declared in a discussion of women in Australian teacher unions: 'Whilst some progress is evident on increased participation of women in teacher unions, levels of representation are still not equal with those of men, nor close to being commensurate with the proportion of women in unions' (1985:19). The employment, administrative and union structures of primary teaching point to a simple conclusion: primary teaching is run mostly by women and is controlled predominantly by men. Tordale and Linfield schools add substance to this conclusion.

Tordale, being a small school with four teachers, does not have the substantial hierarchical structure of Linfield's 25 teachers. However, Tordale does reflect neatly the gender structures of primary teaching in Victoria: 75 per cent women, but with the man as boss. Donna Morton was the school's union sub-branch 'president'.

Linfield was organised into three 'units', each of which represented two or three grade levels. Each unit was staffed by about seven teachers including a 'leader' who was a 'Band Three' level teacher.

Senior to the unit leaders were two 'Band Four' deputy principals and the principal. The unit leaders and above were men. Of the 25 staff in 1984, twelve were men, half of whom occupied the six senior positions in the school. Hence, the Linfield school staff was unusual in its balance of the sexes, but this was offset by a totally male dominated hierarchy. The school's sub-branch of the VTU was controlled by men, with the male president also being on the state executive. Clearly, both Linfield and Tordale primary schools reflect the traditional gender structures of primary teaching. There appears to be little prospect of substantial change. Indeed, the Education Department's policy and planning unit (1985:1-6) suggests that these divisions have not altered fundamentally since 1851, in spite of equal pay in 1971 and the common roll (primary) for men and women teachers in 1972. They observe that, in some respects, matters have worsened in the past sixty years: 'In 1925, 67% of women teachers were allocated to the lowest class, 22% to the second lowest, 7.4% to the third class, 2.4% to the second highest and 0.8% to the highest...In 1984...76% are in the lowest class, 18% in the second lowest, 4% in the third class, 1% in the second highest and 0.9% in the highest' (1985:19).

In 1985, in another move towards devolution, the Ministry of Education introduced an alternative local selection process, whereby school councils can opt to play a role in selecting their new principals. In the first year, only thirty (8 per cent) of the 386 applicants for locally selected primary school principal positions were women. Worse still, after the selection, only two women (4 per cent) were appointed (*Education Victoria* February 1986:3). Given that in 1984, 19 per cent of primary school principals were women, it appears that the policies of devolution and equal opportunity are leading to conflicting practices. The findings in Chapter 3 about the Tordale and Linfield councils lead one to the conclusion that women members would have less influence over the local selection *agenda* than men. Similarly, the council members' *agenda* may, consciously or unconsciously, not include notions of women as potential school principals.

A government can provide policies and guidelines to regulate the practices of school councils, but it cannot immediately overturn the years of lived experience which shape the masculinity and femininity embedded in the culture of a school community. Each member of a school council is an active agent in pressing for his or her own interests. In terms of the local selection of principals, these interests are likely to include the perception that principals, as authority figures, are masculine.

The Linfield and Tordale teachers' backgrounds

Although Miriam Tate's life story contains characteristics which are peculiar to her family, especially due to the remoteness of her rural upbringing, other characteristics, such as meagre family income and the variation in schooling and other opportunities given to boys and girls, are common to other teachers. There was a marked difference between those teachers, such as Miriam Tate, who were approaching 50 years of age or older and those who were under 30. Most primary schools of Linfield's size would have a similar range of ages in their teachers. Tordale too had a similar range, but this is unusual in such a small school. Between the extremes of the teachers' age range lies a generation: more than there is between young teachers and pupils.

Each of the older teachers—except Stephanie Bell, whose parents were teachers—emphasised the difficulties their parents had in keeping them at school beyond the age of fourteen. Teaching was a good career because it meant a bursary for both schooling and tertiary education, and because it represented secure work. The Great Depression of the 1930s had affected their parents' valuing of security of employment in the 1940s and the expansion of education after World War II had confirmed their opinions about the soundness of a teaching career. Some older men had had other careers in mind, but chose teaching because the family could not afford the expense of tertiary education unless a teaching bursary or scholarship was involved. James Porter, who was in his mid-forties and therefore between the younger and older groups, had been keen to become a veterinarian, but his father, a church minister, could not afford the university costs. Teaching also attracted him for what he now sees as the wrong reasons. He thought the holidays and hours of work were good, and the pay satisfactory. Nowadays he believes teachers 'need to be totally committed' to the work, rather than being swayed by the holidays and hours, both of which he considers have declined relatively, through 'community erosion'.

For the older women, teaching was usually the only career presented to them in their families and at school. Mary Thomson came from a large family and was strongly influenced by the prospect of an Education Department bursary to help her continue her schooling and obtain a place at a teachers' college. She obtained a bursary at the age of fourteen and after completing her matriculation trained as a teacher during the early 1950s. Her father worked for a large retailing company and her mother worked at home raising Mary and her younger two sisters and brother. These siblings were to follow her into teaching, although not all immediately after leaving school. By the time Mary Thomson was offered a bursary her mother was sick and the family was 'struggling'. She 'felt that the money would help' and so she accepted. This decision by a fourteen year old was to affect the pattern of the rest of her life: something which was typical of the older teachers.

Although the older teachers did not express any regrets about taking up teaching as a career, it was quite clear that, with the exception of Miriam Tate and Stephanie Bell they had all felt the limitations of their families' financial circumstances. Teaching was selected from the limited options available to them and over the passing years they had come to accept their lot in life with equanimity. For the older women, primary school teaching was a 'natural' aspect of their adult lives, in that it conformed to the views that they, and the social world in which they lived, had of women's work. Some of the older men expressed the view that primary school teaching was 'feminine', both as a career and in terms of the culture of the primary school. James Porter said, 'I see primary school as girl orientated. A lot of the expectations such as neatness, quietness, are ones which girls fit into and boys less so'.

The 'femininity' of primary school teaching was seen by the older male teachers as operating against them in their social relationships with other adults. It was if their work with young children made them less than masculine or even peculiar in the eyes of other adults. Promotion lessened this effect, because authority and power are seen as masculine. Some men of all ages had hankered after secondary teaching, but resorted to primary teaching partly because secondary teaching required higher matriculation grades and more substantial academic study for a particular teaching subject.

The younger teachers made their choices to become primary school teachers without concern for family income. Their parents' and teachers' encouragement had led them to see the completion of secondary schooling as almost inevitable. Only one of these teachers, Carmel Walls, had been to an independent school. They had all been to a teachers' college, or state colleges as they were then called, during the 1970s. With the election of a federal Labor government in 1972, tuition fees at tertiary institutions were abolished. Hence, the financial difficulties for families whose children continued their education were reduced. However, in contrast to several of the older teachers, the younger teachers at Tordale and Linfield came from families where incomes, values and lifestyle were firmly located in the middle class. For example: Donna Morton's father was a state college lecturer and her mother was a secondary teacher; Patrick Kerner's father was a bank manager and his mother worked in the home; Carmel Walls's mother was a painter who also gave private tuition and her father was a quarry manager. The younger teachers, unlike the older teachers, often had mothers who commenced or continued work outside of the home after they, and any brothers or sisters, had begun school. None of the teachers had been cared for by a father at home while their mother worked as the breadwinner.

The younger teachers' career decisions were not always the result of a commitment to work toward teaching. Carmel Walls, for instance, wanted originally to become a secretary; Helen Hansen had had her heart set on being an 'air hostess'. Others, such as Patrick Kerner and Marilyn Carmody, chose to become teachers during their schooling. Patrick Kerner made the decision during his final year at secondary school because he 'likes kids'. Marilyn Carmody thought she could trace her decision back to when she was fifteen and living in Indonesia: 'I don't know really how I came to the decision. It could have been when my grandmother saw me looking after a group of children when we were overseas. And she said to me that I had a real gift for it and she said I should be a teacher. I thought that perhaps I would do that. Dad thought it was a good idea too'.

It is difficult to assess the power of important people, such as parents and grandparents, to influence the career decisions of a young child. It is perhaps all too simple to affirm and then reaffirm, sometimes subtly, sometimes directly, behaviour which is seen as gender appropriate for the boy or girl in question. One wonders how many times Marilyn Carmody demonstrated similar 'gifts' for activities that were seen as inappropriate for her sex, hence were ignored or denounced in some way.

The effect of gender division upon the working lives of the teachers differed markedly between the older and younger teachers. Partly, this was because the younger teachers did not have children of their own, whereas all of the older teachers were parents. The older teachers exhibited the traditional gender differentiation of parenthood. The male teachers pushed on with their careers while their wives committed themselves to parenthood and the seemingly inevitable unpaid domestic labour. The older female teachers had performed the same roles in their own families while their husbands undertook the breadwinning. For Mary Thomson and Stephanie Bell this had meant ten years at home with their, respectively, six and three children. At the time of the research Mary Thomson had been teaching for 22 years and Stephanie Bell for 18 years. They were both on the lowest, Band One, teaching scale. In contrast, their male counterparts, with one exception, were all Band Two teachers or above.

* * *

Rod Miles was between the younger and older age groups. His life was unfolding in a manner which neatly encapsulated the family and career gender relationships that underpin a successful man's primary school teaching career. His wife, Rebecca Miles, an ex-nurse, remained at home to look after their two children, the oldest of whom was a pupil at Tordale. Rod Miles said that he and his wife believed that her responsibility was for their children and also, as the principal's wife, to support him in the community. A vital part of her support centred on her fulfilling their parental responsibilities not only while he worked at the school, but also while he attended meetings and visited parents outside school hours. In addition, she attended school camps with her husband to help supervise the children and to cook. Being a nurse, she also had some other important knowledge and skills to impart. At the November Tordale school council meeting, Rebecca Miles's voluntary work as a teacher's aide at a recent school camp was discussed. Usually, school councils pay for people who work in her capacity, but, as both she and her husband saw this work as part of being a principal's wife, she refused payment. The president, John Sheriff, suggested that a gift would be in order and, although Rod Miles said this was not necessary, the council agreed to provide one. The principal was asked what would be an appropriate gift and he suggested a new frying pan because their present one was rather battered and worn. This was accepted by the council and John Sheriff asked Cynthia Jasper to arrange for the purchase and presentation of a suitable frying pan. At the December council meeting a letter was read out from Rebecca Miles thanking the council for the gift and offering her services at any future school camps.

Rod Miles's career is constructed with his wife's labour. Not only did she release him from the everyday routine of parental responsibility—the routine of feeding, clothing, supervising, transporting, entertaining and supporting—but she also gave him the stable, family-man image upon which he based his dealings with the community. In contrast, a single, male principal may have found working with the Tordale community more difficult.

Teachers' ambitions

The sorts of gender relations embedded in the older teachers' biographies are not passed on from generation to generation carved in tablets of stone. Gender relations are constructed and reconstructed within, for example, family and career contexts, by the people concerned. The biographies of the older teachers were not all identical, as if they had been the products of a powerful and uniform social engineering, but they possessed many common properties, especially in terms of gender, which show that each person's present is a negotiated product of the past.

Miriam Tate's biography is a case in point. Her life contained many traditional gender-related features, however, her path into teaching was one which represented the culmination of a prolonged ambition. As such, it was substantially a fulfilment of her own attempt to direct her later life, rather than a conformity to her original family's circumstance. As a teacher her ambitions were relatively minimal. She wanted to make Band Two in the twelve years or so to her retirement. Her involvement on the school council had whetted her appetite for more administrative responsibility within her career, but she believed that, 'there is a prejudice against older people in the Department' and her opportunities would be few.

However, Miriam Tate's ambitions were in keeping with those of all her female colleagues, irrespective of the ages or years of teaching experience. The one, most senior woman, was a Band Two teacher, and no woman held an ambition to move any higher than this. This finding is consistent with Wentworth's (1979). She found that, amongst final year teacher trainees, women had significantly less ambitious career goals than men. The women teachers at Tordale and Linfield were virtually unanimous in their abhorrence of the possibility of being a principal. Helen Hansen, who had been teaching for nine years, exemplified this view when she said, 'I would never want to be a principal, your head's on the chopping block too much'. There was also the concern that greater seniority meant less teaching and, in particular, losing 'their' class.

The older women teachers had spent several years working in the home supporting their young children and husbands. These years away from their teaching represented a substantial interruption of and often a minor reversal to their careers. They usually returned to teaching lower on the salary scale and feeling out of touch with the changes that had occurred during their absence. These career interruptions typically commenced in their mid to late twenties and lasted for about ten years: a crucial period in most careers. Helen Hansen and Susan O'Reilly were at this age and were seeking Band Two positions. Helen Hansen had divorced recently and moved to Linfield from Melbourne to be nearer to her parents and friends; Susan O'Reilly was unmarried, but had lived in a *de facto* married relationship with a divorcé and his two school age children for three and a half years. She was ambivalent about the prospect of becoming a parent: 'I'd like to have children, but I like the job, getting paid and the friendships with the teachers'. She said of her partner's views about parenthood and her response: 'He thinks that if I had a child I'd more or less have to stay at home with it...I'd stay at home and sweat it out, then come back to work'.

Commonly, the younger women teachers were anticipating such a period for themselves even though none was married and only one, Carmel Walls, was engaged. She said in November 1983 that she planned to continue teaching at Tordale for three years after her marriage in the following January. Then she would have two children, returning to work, perhaps part-time, when they were both at school. Her *agenda* provided for at least seven years away from teaching—which is the length of family leave granted by the Ministry of Education. She had 'no desire to make a big career' of teaching. Within nine months, Carmel Walls had changed her plans. She was becoming dissatisfied at the school and was 'in two minds about coming back next year (1985)'. However, she thought she would work for that year and then, 'I plan after that, towards the end of next year, we're thinking about starting a family'. A few weeks later, Carmel Walls became pregnant and left Tordale during the first half of 1985. She returned to her job at Tordale at the beginning of 1986.

Two younger teachers, Donna Morton at Tordale and Marilyn Carmody at Linfield, were setting their *agendas* to include future relationships with partners which would allow for more equal work and parental responsibilities. However, such *agendas* are founded on their personal relationships with their partners, and not on any specific concern with fulfilling both career and personal ambitions. These two younger women, along with the older Miriam Tate, were the only ones who were critical of existing gender relationships and the effects on their lives. They were the only ones to raise notions of resistance to, and reconstruction of, such relationships in their future lives. Yet even they had no ambition to achieve a senior position in teaching.

* * *

James Porter, a deputy principal at Linfield, with five school appointments in his eighteen years teaching, lamented the fact that he had 'never been in a school where a female member of staff has been in a senior position'. He observed that: 'The men seem to go for the senior roles (and have) career commitment (and the) women are content to teach in the classroom and do that well. It is unfortunate that women don't go for the responsibility, it is always a problem when mothers see their job as second to the family, which fathers don't'. Later he commented, 'There's been equal opportunity in teaching for years, but they don't take it up...I'm in favour of equal opportunity—there has been so much wasted potential—(the effect) on men has got to be good because of the increased competition'.

James Porter is married with three children. His wife, also a teacher, left teaching until their children started school ten years ago. She is a Band One teacher and is improving her qualifications in order to gain promotion. Porter said that he and his wife had shared the domestic labour over the past ten years, but he had 'been personally knocked by men for doing the household chores'. Their son, now at high school, was finding that 'the boys in the community see it as cissy' for him to be required by his parents to share in the household chores with his older sister.

James Porter's views illustrate the various interlocking layers of gender differentiation that beset people who wish to construct a more egalitarian life for themselves. Given that the Porters' work is teaching, the problems of gender differentiation in teaching affect both of their work lives, and here they conform with what is expected of male and female teachers of their ages and years of experience: he the deputy principal and she the junior level teacher. Their attempts to organise their family lives around less traditionally gender-differentiated principles marked something of a departure from the usual pattern. Here the difficulties come to bear on men rather than women, because it is acceptable for women to be in the paid workforce, even if there are some pockets of resistance, but it is less acceptable for men to participate equally in the domestic and parenting chores. Generally, as James Porter found, the opposition came from men, but the depth of prejudice pervades the prevailing culture to such an extent that men are treated as aliens in many contexts where domestic and parenting labour is required. There exist a myriad of social contexts where men are frozen out of participation and responsibility.

At Linfield men, especially senior men, are encumbered with the matters of discipline which arise as a regular part of school life. Porter explained, 'There is an attitude amongst parents that difficult children should be given to a male member of staff... The staff (also) give it to a male, or to a senior member of staff, who, at this school, is male'. The difficulty of breaking this pattern of interlocking gender-differentiation is enormous because the pressures to conform come from all sides: the teachers, the parents, and the pupils who learn to equate discipline with masculinity. The interrelationship between discipline, seniority and masculinity is one which probably encourages male teachers to seek promotion. Because by pursuing promotion to the most 'masculine' levels, such men feel more comfortable amongst people outside of their work. No male teacher overtly expressed this view, but their actions in achieving promotion and maintaining discipline point to this conclusion.

There were only two younger male teachers, which makes it difficult to draw conclusions about the nature of their group. However, their ambitions are worth comparing with those of the younger female teachers. Patrick Kerner's and Steve Weston's career ambitions did not differ greatly from the younger female teachers. In particular, Weston, who was single and had no plans to be otherwise, said that he only wanted to be a successful teacher in a small rural school in an area such as the Mornington Peninsula: a fashionable rural/urban fringe coastal area on the south-eastern outskirts of Melbourne. Kerner was recently married and looking for promotion to Band Two. His wife worked in the insurance business and they planned to have children 'in a couple of years' after they had 'enjoyed gallivanting around and overseas holidays'. A direct comparison exists between Patrick Kerner and Carmel Walls. They were of similar ages, had trained almost simultaneously at the local college, were recently married and planned to have children. Even allowing for Kerner's minimal ambition, by the time they are both parents of school age children their careers are likely to have diverged considerably. Kerner was not contemplating family leave, but Walls was; although she did return to work after her first child more quickly than she had planned. Assuming they both have at least two children, then in a few years' time Patrick Kerner will be looking for another promotion to Band Three and Carmel Walls will have returned to Band One. Such decisions are exercised by mothers and fathers as a matter of choice, albeit with some heavy social pressure to conform to traditional parenting and breadwinning patterns. The choice exists for the younger teachers because, since 1983, either parent is eligible for family leave.

The point where the careers of men and women teachers begin to diverge is when they establish relationships with partners that lead to marriage. All of the (male) senior teachers were married and parents; all of the women, apart from the younger ones, were either married or divorced, and all the older women were parents. Those teachers who had married or were contemplating doing so, said that their initial consideration of marriage was blended with thoughts about parenthood. Once the decision was made to marry and, almost inevitably, to have children, then the teachers' career ambitions became more clearly defined. The men recognised this point as one at which the thought of promotion became more pressing. For them, promotion meant a superior breadwinning capability, which became a practical manifestation of the fulfilment of their responsibility to their spouse and children. The opposite was the case for the women; their careers became secondary to their planned parenthood and the fulfilment of their responsibility to their children.

These research findings about the relationships between gender, marriage, family and teachers' unfolding career ambitions accord with evidence from other studies. For example, Ollerenshaw and Flude (1974) also found that British women teachers generally gave up teaching not upon marriage, but at the onset of parenthood. Lortie, in a study of North American teachers, found complementary evidence in relation to male and female teachers' perceptions of career and work rewards (1975:82-98). It is difficult to see how the current career structure of primary teaching in Victoria could lead to such a career discrepancy. Certainly, previous parental leave regulations mitigated against men participating in, and taking responsibility for, their young children and, thereby, heaped the responsibility on women. Such discriminatory leave provisions powerfully set the *agenda* for people's thinking and discussion about careers and family life. As these previous discriminatory leave provisions and practices—and they continue in most occupations—were deeply embedded in the gender structures of society, then the *agenda* shaped by the Education Department was in harmony with the broader culture. This doubtless left teachers virtually without room to cultivate and shape their career and parenting practices in a fair and equitable manner.

However, even with the current family leave provisions in the Ministry of Education, women teachers who become parents always face a greater disruption to their careers than men, simply because they do the childbearing. Likewise, the patchy provision of good childcare facilities makes it difficult for parents, especially mothers, to return to work before their children reach school age. Also, as Acker argues, conceptions of career and career rewards are delineated along masculine lines throughout class structured societies (1983:123-139). Hence, when comparing men and women teachers' career ambitions, it must be recognised that the terms of that comparison are linked to a career structure which was organised by men in their own interests (see Lewin and Olesen, 1981).

Teachers and their children

All primary school teachers 'have' children: most are parents and all have their daily working lives centred around children. Many primary school teachers see more of the waking lives of their pupils than do the pupils' parents, especially fathers; likewise they often see more of the waking lives of their pupils than they see of their own children. Given that teachers, as parents, shape their career and parental ambitions and practices in terms of the broader social and employment provisions which apply, then the consequences of their decisions also bear upon their own children and pupils. The extent to which their beliefs and practices are sexist will have a direct effect on the socialisation they impart, both at home and school.

Miriam Tate's case showed how the influences of her parents, grandparents and others bore upon her life, and how eventually she was to be in a position to influence the lives of her own children and pupils. In effect, this 'wheel' has turned through four generations and left its own unique 'track'. However, the teachers' actions towards the children in their lives demonstrate the ever present structuring processes which keep the 'wheel' on the 'road'. Teachers use their own understanding of gender in their work or when, as parents, they face the responsibilities of caring for their own children. It is important to see the extent to which these understandings reverberate back through their lives and career histories, and reflect the broader social structural conditions which shaped them.

In keeping with previous research findings (Evans, 1982a), the Linfield and Tordale teachers described characteristics which they believed distinguished male and female pupils from one another. James Porter's belief that primary schools are 'girl orientated' with their emphasis on 'neatness' and 'quietness', is a continuation of the argument that primary schooling is a feminine world. His view sidesteps the domination of primary schooling by men, such as Porter, and focuses on supposed feminine traits to explain how boys are less able to adjust to primary schooling. This argument helps to 'explain' what all the teachers saw as the more unruly behaviour from boys and the greater, using Porter's words, 'remedial treatment' given to boys. The teachers explained the types of unruly behaviour which they experienced in their work. There was a common view that boys are, in Linfield teacher Tony Sgroi's words, 'more physical' and girls, 'more verbal' in their aggressive wrong-doings. This physical – verbal dichotomy has its ramifications throughout the curriculum and the classroom, as is demonstrated in Chapters 6 and 7 respectively. It also appeared to be transposed by the teachers into a perceived dichotomy of manual/mechanical versus passive/mental, between boys and girls respectively, when discussing their general interests and abilities.

There are, however, apparent contradictions between the teachers' expressed perceptions of the children. They both observed the products, as they saw them, of traditional gender differentiation, and also intruded their received egalitarian views in such matters. So, the teachers commonly provided their observations of the gender differentiated children's actions which surrounded them, but also expressed regrets that this is still the case. All teachers espoused egalitarian principles in theory (see Evans, 1982a), but the extent to which such principles shaped their own lives and actions was another matter. Even their perceptions of children's behaviour contained apparent inconsistencies. For example, in spite of the view that boys are more physical in their behaviour, in relation to sport, the teachers had differing opinions about physical abilities of boys and girls. Some saw the girls as being better than the boys, and others stated the contrary. Likewise, some teachers saw girls as being more 'verbally' adept than boys, others saw no difference.

These differences may be partly accounted for by the common perception that the age of the children affected the differences between boys and girls. Tony Sgroi went so far as to say: 'Girls in grade six are a race apart almost (from the boys). They are more mature physically and emotionally than boys'. Susan O'Reilly said: 'It's only when they (the boys) get older that they start all this macho business'. As might have been expected, those teachers whose work was more often centred upon the younger grades generally saw fewer differences between boys and girls than those whose work was more often centred upon the older grades. However, the reasons for the apparently more marked differences between the boys and girls as they grew older are important to ascertain. If accepted at face value, the teachers' views imply that boys and girls become increasingly different during, if not because of, their schooling. Perhaps their views are coloured by the demonstrably gender-segregated structure of their own work and family relationships. Hence, as they see the children growing closer to their own adult selves, they are working to gender structure the children accordingly.

Some of the teachers, in particular, Stephanie Bell, Ted Symes, James Porter, Mary Thomson and Miriam Tate, had adult children of their own. It is worth seeing how these adult children reflected their parents' backgrounds. Miriam Tate's children, as was noted previously, had left school and were in the workforce. Whereas Tate had been forced to end her correspondence schooling in order to work on the farm while her brother was required to continue his schooling, her son had resisted schooling and voluntarily left to obtain an apprenticeship. She wanted her children to go to university, but they chose work. Her daughter had completed all her schooling and could have continued to university, but chose a job in a government bureaucracy instead. The daughter had been promoted several times and at the time of our research was earning a larger salary than her mother. Stephanie Bell had two adult children, a daughter who was a clerical assistant in a private company and a son who was an electrical apprentice. Almost without exception these teachers' remaining adult children, all daughters, were studying at university in the arts, law and languages areas. Some were likely to become secondary school teachers.

The teachers' adult children reflect the current shifts toward equal opportunities for women. In comparison with their teacher-mothers at the same age, most daughters were in a better position to pursue an independent life and a career. They are similar to the younger teachers, except that their university degrees provide wider opportunities. However, no daughter was studying in the traditional 'male' areas of science and technology. The only two adult sons of the older teachers had apprenticeships in traditional 'male' occupations.

With such small numbers of teachers in the study having adult children it is impossible to draw any general conclusions other than to say that the difference between the generations of women appeared to be quite significant. This difference seems largely a result of changes over the past forty years or so to the families and their educational experiences. Such changes have occurred within the context of broader social and other developments during this period. In the following chapter, the parents and families of the children are considered, providing another view of gender relationships across generations.

5 The parents

Families, like schools, are where generations meet. Both involve the upbringing and care of the younger generation. For schools, the task is to equip the rising generation with the skills, knowledge and values required for the perpetuation of society. Families do a similar job, but their most distinguishing feature, as Engels (1968) noted, is human reproduction: physically producing the next generation. Traditionally, in industrial societies, family formation commences with marriage and is realised with the birth of a child. Families are also formed and continue in other ways, with or without marriage, sometimes with one parent, or with existing children. Families, sexuality and human reproduction are influenced by religious and moral traditions, which feminists and others argue are oppressive, especially towards women and girls (Summers, 1975). These traditions enforce the belief that the only appropriate adult life is within a monogamous, heterosexual, married relationship producing one or a few children. As I argued in the previous chapter, this is the sort of relationship expected of principals in their communities. Also, as Bryson (1984) notes, male domination is the rule in families.

The birth of a young child ushers in an era of parenting which often extends until, and occasionally into, that child's adulthood. The bulk of this parenting, especially in the child's earliest years, falls upon the mother; in effect parenting becomes mothering. The ideology of motherhood morally attaches women to their children as firmly as if the umbilical cord remained intact. Badinter (1981), Mitchell (1971), Oakley (1974b) and Wearing (1984) criticise this ideology—espoused by many, especially Bowlby (1953, 1971)—and demonstrate its links with women's oppression and the maintenance of patriarchal relationships.

Parenthood is not only gender divided adult work; it is also a gender divided practice. Children are reared according to their sex, although this has possibly diminished in recent years. This practice is accomplished partly by the children learning, and accepting as given, the gender relationships they see in their own family lives. The extent to which adult work—breadwinning, parenting and domestic—is gender structured is seen and lived through by children in their families. Children's first understanding of parenthood, and also domestic and breadwinning work, is structured in this way. In effect, children's everyday practical experience of adult work sets the *agenda* for their thinking and learning about their own future adult work. Because this *agenda* is gender structured, their subsequent thinking, learning and behaviour has a strong and enduring gender basis.

From school age children are exposed to the broader *gender agenda* of the school, which meshes neatly, if not perfectly, with the ways the adults in schools organise their work, and with the form of schooling they experience in the classroom. Although adults gender-structure the *agenda* of children's lives, it remains for the children to interpret and use this *agenda* according to their social and intellectual skills.

Parents' work: breadwinning

Every family is dependent on income in order to sustain its existence. This income comes usually from paid work, investments or pensions, accruing to the family members who are beyond the school leaving age, which in Australia is usually fifteen. However, often not every family member is a breadwinner, mostly because of the need for domestic and parenting work, and sometimes because of unemployment or further education.

Appendixes 9.2 and 9.3 show ages of men and women in the Linfield and Tordale workforces in 1976 and 1981. These tables show that across all ages and both communities approximately one third of the workforce are women. Due to the tiny population of Tordale, small variations in numbers can produce large changes in the percentages of men and women in different age categories, however, it is clear that in 1976 and 1981, for both Tordale and Linfield, the 15-19 year olds possessed the most stable and equal work participation rate across the sexes. Even here, at between 43 and 45 per cent, the women were 10 per cent below the men and 5 per cent below equivalence. The real decline in women's participation in the workforce comes in their early twenties when marriage and childbirth are most common. These figures show how clear the links are between the gender divisions in family work and participation in the paid workforce. The evidence indicates that some women return to paid work in their thirties, but that older women either remain at home or only return temporarily to work.

The five year span between the figures presented in Appendixes 9.2 and 9.3 coincides with the commencement of the international push to improve the position of women. In Linfield, which has a workforce over sixteen times greater than Tordale, during this period there was a 2 per cent decrease in the participation rate of women in the Linfield workforce. Given that any improvement in the position of women requires changes to be made to both male and female participation in work and family life, then in the case of paid employment for Linfield women, life had become slightly worse. Evans and Nation recorded in May 1980 that in this area of the Latrobe Valley, 'there were only 17 job vacancies for women in the administrative and sales category and 564 women registered as unemployed applicants for these jobs'. It was concluded that, 'the "female" labour market is under threat from...the recession, the "collapse" of manufacturing industry and technological change' (1984:230). The parents of the Linfield and Tordale primary school children were mainly in the 15-19 through to 30-34 age groups in 1976 and in the 20-24 through to 35-39 age groups in 1981. This is the age range that encompasses the period when women both leave and some later seek to rejoin the workforce. Clearly, by 1981 it had become very difficult for most such women to rejoin the workforce.

One of the ways women choose to rejoin the workforce is through part-time work. Appendixes 9.4, 9.5, 9.6 and 9.7 show the distribution of personal incomes for the Tordale and Linfield communities for 1976 and 1981. Approximately 80 per cent of the lowest income earners are women which suggests that a considerable proportion of these women are in low income, part-time work. Conversely, women comprise a tiny percentage of the highest income earners in Linfield and are not represented at all in this category at Tordale. The Tordale tables (9.6 and 9.7) show that in 1976 there were no income earners in the highest category and no women in the highest two categories. However, by 1981 there were nine men in the highest category and six women in the second category. This reflects the Blockie move into the community as farming waned. Also it says something about the school staff during this period. In particular, it means that in 1976 the principal, who would have been in the highest income category, and any other women staff were not living in Tordale, because all Tordale teachers would be in the second highest income category on the basis of their salary. However, during our research we recorded that two of the teachers lived in Tordale at the time of the 1981 census, hence, two out of the six highest paid women were teachers at the school.

The percentages of Linfield women in the two highest income categories increased slightly from 1976 to 1981, but, likewise, the two lowest categories increased in their proportions of women. Therefore, while there was a small shift towards equality between the sexes in the two upper income categories there was a corresponding shift away in the lowest. This is borne out in the Tordale tables with large increases in the proportions of women in the lowest income categories and in the second highest category. Perhaps this suggests that the better qualified women, such as teachers, are becoming increasingly distanced from their less qualified sisters, not only in terms of income, but also in terms of their corresponding social and political power.

The educational levels of women in the 1976 and 1981 censuses support this argument. In 1976 all of the Tordale women had left school by age 16 and only 4 (11 per cent) achieved post school qualifications: two trade certificates and two technician certificates. However, in 1981 21 per cent had left school after 16 and the proportion of women with post-school qualifications had almost doubled to 21 per cent: three had diplomas (two of whom were the Tordale teachers) and five had trade or technician certificates. This increase in the educational levels of the Tordale women is an indication of the significant Blockie influx during this period. The pattern was more stable at Linfield where in 1976 86 per cent of the women had left school by age 16 compared with 83 per cent in 1981. The proportion with post school qualifications had increased slightly from 11 per cent to 12 per cent.

In 1976, 13 per cent of Tordale men and 10 per cent of Linfield men had continued their schooling beyond age 16; by 1981 these proportions had increased to 16 and 19 per cent respectively. Especially in Linfield, the men's schooling levels are close to those for women. However, the differences are more marked for post-school qualifications. In 1976, 24 per cent of Tordale men and 22 per cent of Linfield men had post-school qualifications, by 1981 these proportions had increased to 25 and 37 per cent respectively. Approximately 80 per cent of these post-school qualifications are trade certificates, which are obtained usually through an apprenticeship after leaving school at age 15 or 16.

With the exception of trades such as hairdressing, the majority of trades are seen as 'men's work'. In mining and industrial communities there are opportunities for boys to pursue such trades as boilermaking, fitting and turning or instrument making in addition to the more common trades of carpentry, plumbing or electrical work. The Linfield figures exemplify the consequences of the gender-divided apprenticeship system where between two and three times as many men as women have post-school qualifications. Nearly all the post-school qualifications provide access to particular sections of the labour market from which the unqualified are excluded. This applies, not only to trade and technician certificates, but also to the other qualifications, such as teaching diplomas and engineering degrees, held by a few members of the Linfield and Tordale communities.

Three paths from school to adulthood

Jane Peters left school on her fifteenth birthday. School was a drag, so there was no point in finishing year ten, and anyway, she had lined up a job in a dry cleaners which was much more interesting. 'A lot of girls might want to do what I did. Work for a while after (leaving) school and then get married. That seems to be the ambition of a lot of girls. I guess that's changing now, with more careers'. After marriage, paid work ceased as quickly as school had when she turned fifteen; she isn't intending to earn another pay packet again. Jane Peters has 'been just a mum for the past six years' to her three sons. Her husband works on a Bass Strait oil rig and so he regularly spends several weeks away from home. She thinks that her three sons 'need (education) more than girls' and so she will encourage them to obtain qualifications 'because it will help get jobs'. Her school experiences temper her aspirations for her sons: 'I hope they grow up happy and do what they want to do. (I) hope they get a good education on the way. But if they don't want to stay at school then I'm not going to force them because I didn't like school myself'.

Brian Garden left school at thirteen and a half to join the navy as a cadet. At seventeen he had had enough: 'I failed Seamanship and you don't have much of a career in the navy if you fail that. Anyway me and the navy were starting to go our separate ways. It was hard to cope with the thoughtless discipline'. At seventeen he joined a bank in Melbourne and after two years he was transferred to the Latrobe Valley. He married and later took a job in the accounts department of a large organisation in the valley. After six years in accounts he moved into industrial relations work and, despite his lack of educational qualifications, he progressed in his career by accepting opportunities as they arose. His three children, the youngest is in grade five at Linfield, are principally cared for by his wife, who has remained outside of the workforce since their first son was born sixteen years ago.

Andrew Masters is a local boy who completed year twelve at high school and graduated in engineering from a nearby college in 1972. He married a local girl who became a teacher in the same high school she attended as a student. Unlike Jane Peters and Brian Garden, Andrew Masters is amongst the small percentage of people who continued their schooling past the age of sixteen and the even smaller percentage who graduated with degrees. He worked as an engineer for two years during which time he decided to train as a teacher in Melbourne. He returned to the Latrobe Valley to teach, but found that he and the school 'had major philosophical differences'. He explained that, 'My expectations of the school and what I found at the school were not what I wanted them to be...I had a lot of trouble reconciling myself to those differences...Teaching is not really what I wanted to do'. In 1976 he returned to engineering. Initially he joined the company for which his mother had worked until her marriage. He now works in the same organisation as Brian Garden. His wife, Miriam, has just returned to teaching after a seven year break to have and look after their three children. Andrew and Miriam Masters are people with deep roots in the Latrobe Valley and are able to call upon a range of contacts and connections to smooth their path through life.

In their range of school experiences and gender segregated work histories, Jane Peters, Brian Garden and Andrew Masters represent typical Linfield parents. However, they are exceptional in their involvement with the school. Jane Peters is a school council member and president of the parents' club. Brian Garden has been a member of the school council for many years, most of them as president, a position he held until 1984 when Andrew Masters became president. Despite his reservations about schooling, Andrew Masters became a member of the Linfield school council soon after his first child was enrolled.

Andrew Masters and Brian Garden develop their careers while their wives, like Jane Peters, perform the majority of the domestic and parenting labour. Miriam Masters exemplifies the few women in the Linfield and Tordale communities who possess educational qualifications that provide them with access to specific sections of the labour market (see Appendixes 9.8 and 9.9). She was able to return to teaching after a period of domestic and parenting work by virtue of her qualifications as a secondary teacher. Appendix 9.8 shows that Linfield women, such as Miriam Masters, were equally represented with men in the professional and technical employment categories, even though they comprised less than one third of the total workforce.

In the trade occupations, where many of the men who left school at the minimum age gained their post-school qualifications, Linfield and Tordale women comprise only 7 per cent of the workforce. Trades are the largest single employment category for both communities and this has increased between 1976 and 1981, as has the total working population. Eight per cent of the Linfield and Tordale workforces in 1981 were in the professional and technical employment categories and, although this only represents a small increase from 7 per cent in Linfield, it marks a doubling of the proportion of such people at Tordale. The decline in the numbers of people working in farming is quite dramatic. In Linfield, between 1976 and 1981, the drop was from 5 to 2 per cent, whereas in Tordale, the fall was from 22 to 3 per cent.

In the three instances where there were dramatic changes in the occupational structure—both the Tordale and Linfield farming decreases, and the Tordale professional and technical increase—it is worth noting the place of women in these changes. The decline in farming brought with it the complete removal of women from these occupations. Conversely, the increase in professional and technical work at Tordale was largely brought about by the increase in women from zero to two. Our research at Tordale school shows that these two women were the teachers: Donna Morton and Stephanie Bell.

Clerical and sales occupations are the only ones where women clearly outnumber men, although women also show some numerical dominance in services and sports. In 1981, 74 per cent of the Linfield and all of the Tordale clerical workers were women, and in sales work, 59 and 78 per cent were the respective proportions. Overall, sales and clerical work maintained stable proportions of the increased Linfield and Tordale workforces. Together these occupations represent respectively 19 and 22 per cent of Linfield and Tordale adults' paid work.

The following table (5.1) shows the occupations of fathers of children enrolling at Tordale school in 1964, 1974 and 1984. We obtained this information from the school's records and, although by 1984 both mothers' and fathers' occupations were recorded at enrolment, unfortunately, this had not been so ten and twenty years before. Linfield, partly because it is a younger school, did not possess records for these years. The twenty year record includes mention of the occupation of a 1964 father who is now the grandparent of a girl who enrolled in 1984. The occupations shown in the tables stem from those described by the parents when enrolling their children, usually at age five.

Table 5.1 shows the decline in farming over twenty years, to the extent that no father of a child enrolling in 1984 was a farmer. The 1964 fathers were mostly working class with their work centred

Table 5.1 Fathers' occupations for children enrolling at Tordale school, 1964, 1974 and 1984.

Occupation	1964	1974	1984
Farmer	5	4	–
Labourer	2	1	1
Police/fire officer	2	–	–
Pulp cutter	2	1	–
Carter/driver	2	1	1
Contractor/operator	1	2	–
Engineer/scientist	–	–	2
Supervisor	–	–	3
Trades	–	–	1
Teacher	–	1	1
Totals	14	10	9

around agriculture and forestry. In 1974 the fathers' occupations were often in the developing industries of the region. By 1984 the fathers were mainly middle class: the Blockies had arrived! No father was recorded as being unemployed or as being employed in 'home duties'; they were all breadwinners.

Table 5.2, which shows the occupations of all the parents at Tordale school in 1983, provides further evidence of the fathers' total involvement in breadwinning. Seventeen mothers (37 per cent) were also breadwinners. Table 5.3 gives the equivalent figures for Linfield school where fathers are again the major breadwinners with only 50 mothers (17 per cent) in the paid workforce. The predominantly working-class backgrounds of the families is also clear. However, it is the gender division in the workforce between 'home duties' and breadwinning which is most marked, especially the absence of fathers in 'home duties'. Such a widespread division relies on a multitude of similar divisions in male and female relationships throughout the community. Usually these relationships are based on marriage. The Tordale parents were each in traditional married relationships and, as Table 5.4 shows, so were the majority (82 per cent) of the Linfield parents. In fact, 98 per cent of the Linfield parents had experienced marriage.

Parents' work: domestic labour

Marriage is a point in adults' lives when an *agenda* for future breadwinning and domestic labour is set. Sometimes the *agenda* is formed in the preceding period, especially if the partners have lived

Table 5.2 Parents' occupations for children attending Tordale school, 1983.

Occupation	mothers	fathers
Home duties	29	–
Unskilled/semi-skilled	2	14
Professional/semi-professional	5	9
Farming	1	5
Clerical/administrative	5	1
Managerial/supervisory	3	1
Trades	–	16
Retail assistant	1	–
Totals	46	46

Table 5.3 Parents' occupations for children attending Linfield school, 1983.

Occupation	mothers	fathers
Home duties	243	–
Unskilled/semi-skilled	20	131
Clerical/administrative	9	14
Trades	–	69
Professional/semi-professional	14	15
Managerial/supervisory	4	21
Unemployed/pensioner[a]	–	4
Not stated	3	1
Totals	293	255

Note: [a]A few mothers who gave home duties as their occupation may have received a pension.

Table 5.4 Parents' status for children attending Linfield school, 1983.

Marital status	number
Married	246
Separated	42
Divorced	8
Others[a]	6
Total	302

Note: [a]Includes: guardianship, unmarried etc.

together, but marriage brings a legal bond which includes recognition of the different types of work the partners contribute. Ironically, this legal recognition is most visibly manifest when marriages end, either in death or divorce, but it is also evident in taxation and social welfare legislation. However, domestic work provided in the home is generally ignored or given a low priority by policy makers, economists and others. It is difficult to assess the economic value of domestic labour because it operates almost entirely outside of the paid labour market, but the cumulative total would surely outstrip even the largest public and private organisations (see Baldock and Cass, 1983).

Tables 5.2 and 5.3 show that only mothers, 63 per cent at Tordale and 83 per cent at Linfield, said that 'home duties' was their occupation. However, the volume of domestic labour performed within any family is such that most, if not all, members contribute in some form. But our evidence from the group interviews with pupils shows that mothers are seen by their children as the major contributors of domestic labour. This was the case whether their mothers worked outside of the home, full or part-time, or not. Almost without exception, the children see themselves, and sometimes their siblings, as the second largest contributors of domestic labour. Claudia (grade four, Linfield) estimated that, 'Mum does most of the work, then I come second, my sister third and my Dad comes last'. Usually, fathers are seen as minor contributors, either of necessity or out of laziness. For example, Bella (grade three, Linfield) concluded, 'My Dad can't because he's at work all the time'. Steven (grade three, Linfield) said, 'My Dad doesn't (do any housework). He just sits by the fire and puts his nose into the paper'.

In most cases the domestic work performed by fathers is washing or drying dishes. However, this is complicated by a gender division of domestic labour, whereby jobs such as mowing lawns, cutting firewood or house maintenance are seen as men's work. In a few cases mothers did this work, but not without some children seeing it as strange. When Carol (grade three, Tordale) said that her mother mowed the lawns another member of the group, Brian, enquired as to what was wrong with her father! He added, 'I know something... ladies don't help outside and they do all the stuff inside.' Given the gender relationships evident in the case study on the ride-on mower in Chapter 3, maybe one can see Brian as presidential material for a future Tordale school council!

It was clear that the *agenda* for the parents' everyday lives was largely ordered by the traditional sexual divisions of work and family life. However, these *agenda* are modified continually to meet the general and specific needs and interests of the people concerned. Hence, a particular parent's skills or interests in, say, cooking or gardening, are likely to affect the distribution of those forms of labour in the family. So fathers help with the cooking or mothers help in the garden if each is competent in or enjoys this work. When mothers are sick or injured then the children say that their fathers usually increase their work in the home. Some children believe it is important for men and boys to be competent at domestic jobs so that they could stand-in when the womenfolk are sick or injured, or as Nigel (grade six, Linfield) observed, 'because if they (husband and wife) split up, then the bloke's going to have a hard time'.

Similarly, if mothers work to contribute to the family income then the constraints of their work are seen by the children to affect the organisation of domestic labour. Fathers performed more domestic work when the mothers earned a wage, however, the mothers still continued to do most of the domestic work, something which is recorded in other contexts (e.g. Meisner, 1975). What galled a lot of children was that they had to do more work in the home when both their parents worked. Therefore, we found some resistance from children to the idea of mothers working because they did not want any more domestic work. Material benefits remained unrecognised, as did any intrinsic rewards their mothers gained from being in the paid workforce. As is shown in the following chapter, such things are recognised as important when the children talk about their future adult lives.

The remarkable feature of the pupil interviews is the constant degradation of domestic labour and the mothers who perform it. The belief is that housework is boring, mundane and tedious, and that their mothers should do it. Duane (grade four, Tordale) said, 'cleaning up's a woman's job'. Carl (grade five, Linfield) was of the opinion that, 'women should stick to the housework...otherwise the kids have to do all the work...The Dads get the money and the women don't have to get the money. They can just stay at home...'. William (grade five, Linfield) agreed, 'I reckon the men should go out to work and the women should clean up the house'. The girls, especially the older ones, were less dogmatic in their opinions, probably because they were beginning to understand the consequences for their adult lives. However, they found it difficult to think of domestic work as being anything other than women's work. Cheryl (grade five, Tordale) believed that domestic work 'should be a team thing' between men and women. 'The men should do some of the ladies' work. No it's not really ladies' work, but kind of washing the dishes...because if the lady gets sick and the men haven't had the experience, the men would never be able to take over'.

Gaskell, in a study of Canadian seventeen and eighteen year olds, found some similar contradictions between some girls' perceptions of 'the domestic ideology...(of) putting family responsibilities first is the perferred pattern for a woman' and those who see that, 'paid work provides status, money and independence' (1983). The Linfield and Tordale mothers are in an impossible position. Domestic work is an essential component of family life which, according to the domestic ideology, falls to them to fulfil. However, its essential nature does not mitigate against this work being seen as low-status and the mothers being perceived accordingly. When they are involved in paid work their children think little of it, even though breadwinning is often seen by these children as a sufficient reason for their fathers to be absolved from most domestic labour. Previously, it was noted that Miriam Tate experienced similar difficulties when she became a student teacher.

The domestic ideology which binds women to domestic labour banishes men to the 'do it yourself' labour on the house and garden. Linfield deputy principal, James Porter, found this to be the case when he assumed a substantial share of the family's domestic labour. Tolson (1977) sees this as one of the elements which are beyond the 'limits of masculinity' in contemporary patriarchal societies. The fact that no father is solely involved in domestic labour and the majority of mothers are, is testimony to the power of the gender-structuring processes which have shaped the lives of these people. Those mothers who are occupied in paid work remained burdened with the *responsibility* for the domestic labour, although some of the work was given to the children or accepted by their menfolk.

Parents' work: parenting

As Gaskell's (1983) research shows, the domestic ideology contains the requirement that women take the major responsibility for parenting; as was stated earlier, in effect parenthood becomes motherhood. However, parenting can be seen as a particular kind of work, taking place mostly in the home, which generates a demand for increased domestic labour. Some of the increased domestic work, for example, the preparation of infant foods or the washing of nappies, impinge directly on parenting. Whereas other increases in domestic work are more remote from parenting and merely reflect an increase in the number of people in the home who generate domestic work, such as washing and ironing clothes or cleaning.

Domestic labour exists as the responsibility of females irrespective of whether they are mothers or not. In any setting where they live, be it as children in a family, sharing a flat with peers, cohabiting with a male partner or in marriage, then the responsibility for domestic labour falls largely to them. Becoming a parent adds another, interconnected, layer to this responsibility. The Linfield and Tordale mothers assume this responsibility without question. Even the mothers at Tordale, who proved themselves to be both influential and occasionally resistant to the principal and men on the school council, never questioned their burden of parenthood. Before and after school, it is typically mothers who shepherd their younger children to and fro. They occasionally help with reading in class or accompany a school excursion or camp. They also, under the guise of being a 'good parent', perform 'domestic' labour in the school canteen and at camps, fetes or working bees. At Linfield, as a gesture of gratitude for the staff's efforts during the year, some of the mothers provide them with a morning tea. However, this represents an event that fathers hardly would consider and even if they did, they would have the women do the catering and washing up. The structure of school life allocates more of this form of 'domestic' labour to mothers. In so doing it helps to reinforce the domestic ideology and set the *agenda* for its reproduction in their children.

There is a strong view amongst the parents and children that mothers should not be engaged in breadwinning when their children are below school age. This accords with the teachers' views, although, in practice, the teachers are not always as tolerant of working parents when they want to arrange interviews or use parents' unpaid labour at school. Some mothers see their commitment to parenthood as requiring the renunciation of breadwinning entirely. As Daphne Wearing from Tordale affirmed, 'Once I had committed myself to having children, that was it. They were priority number one.' She has been married for twenty years, has three children and gave up her job as a typist seventeen years ago.

The children's views demonstrate how the gender relationships of their parents and teachers are being used as the *agenda* for their future adult lives. Sonya (grade five, Tordale) believes she would only return to work 'if they (her future children) had gone to school'. Her peer, Peter, concluded, 'I'd be allright because the wife would be able to look after the children'. However, some of the older children are more circumspect; they see marriage and children as less inevitable, and some girls would prefer fewer children than their mothers. There is also a belief amongst the children that their fathers are incompetent parents, that is, incompetent at the child-care work that their mothers perform as a matter of routine. Russell (1979) found that in families where both parents shared responsibilities for breadwinning, domestic work and parenting, fathers proved to be competent at the child-care tasks. However, in the gender structured Tordale and Linfield communities, this is not the case. Some fathers are relegated to the position of 'baby-sitters' in their children's minds. Veronica (grade six, Linfield) dislikes her mother going to work in the evenings, 'because Dad has to baby-sit, and on the nights when Mum comes home grumpy, Dad gets grumpy and the kids are squeezed in the middle'. Lorraine (grade six, Tordale) sees her father as incompetent at an important child-care task: 'When my Dad changes my brother's nappies he can't do it. And once he was sick. And I had to do it because my Mum was out.' Tony listened to Lorraine's account and concluded, 'I don't think I could handle nappies if I tried.'

Tony's background is interesting in this context. He has three older sisters who assist with domestic work, but Tony is expected to do little at home. However, he helps his father around the farm and when asked about his future career he replied, 'I suppose I've already got a job. I'm taking over the farm.' Tony's family can be seen as the archetypal Tordale Farmer family. Conservative gender relationships prevail and Tony, the youngest child and the only male, would be 'taking over' the farm. The daughters are being raised to domestic labour and dependence on male breadwinners. The irony is that Tony believes changing nappies is beyond his capabilities and yet there are many farming tasks which he is likely to help with, such as treating fly-struck sheep, which make changing the dirtiest nappy seem quite bearable. However, Tony knew these two jobs were allocated according to sex, the one in keeping with his 'masculinity', the other not.

The fathers who participate in working bees, attend parent-teacher meetings or become school councillors, see these activities as part of being good parents. They think poorly of fathers who do not help in such school activities and, particularly at Linfield, this is a source of resentment. However, in equating parenthood with these forms of school activity, fathers are able to shift their parental responsibility from the home, to the more masculine territory of maintenance work at school or attending meetings. Within their families such fathers are able to absent themselves from what little parenting they do at weekends or during evenings, in order to perform what are recognised as important tasks. In this way the power wielded by men on the Tordale and Linfield councils is further legitimised in the home and helps to structure the parenting *agenda* for their children.

It is also possible that the fathers' perceived lack of competence contributes to the mothers' lack of participation in school council and evening meetings. Mothers are tied to their children in the evenings and need to make a special arrangement with the fathers to 'baby-sit' in order to attend evening meetings. If the fathers lack parenting competence, or they manoeuvre to prevent their women-folk from being outside the home, then mothers are likely to decide that committing themselves to regular evening meetings is unwise or more trouble than it is worth.

Concluding comment

Parenting, domestic work and breadwinning are crucial and interdependent elements of most adult lives. In families, this interdependence is largely disentangled and allocated to men and women according to traditional patterns of gender differentiation. Even where women participate in breadwinning work they do so substantially in traditional 'female' occupations in the clerical, secretarial and retailing areas. The children of the Tordale and Linfield families show how this gender differentiation affects their everyday lives and how it is providing the *agenda* for the thinking, decisions and actions they make about their own lives.

In the final section of this book the children are the focus. The schools are presented as the sites in which the children 'work'. Such sites have been planned, organised and operated by adults as part of their work. Many of these adults impinge directly on the children's lives at home or school and, in so doing, provide them with a practical, living *gender agenda* with which they mould their future practice. We have seen in this and previous chapters that the *gender agenda* is evident in the lives of the teachers and parents, and that it is deeply embedded in the thinking, decisions and actions which are made by these people throughout their lives. It remains for us to understand the extent to which the children are adopting the *agenda* that surrounds them, and whether they are developing a new *agenda* for themselves.

Part 2 The children's world of school

6 Pupil knowledge and school *agendas*

The family worlds into which children are born envelop them and become their own. The ways parents and any older siblings live their everyday existences become the *agenda* for the children's own activities. Gender, as has been shown previously, is a major shaping influence on the lives of parents and so it follows that gender also becomes increasingly important in the lives of young children. Gender becomes an issue in everyone's life from the minute they are born; trivial symbols of masculinity and femininity such as the colours of baby clothes, or the designs and words of congratulation cards to mothers, or even the violation of males through circumcision, signify the commencement of a process of gender differentiation which accompanies them to the grave.

In the family, these processes are not so much imposed by external institutions, such as hospitals, as lived out through the lives of family members. The gender differentiation of parenting, domestic and breadwinning labour becomes the context in which young children grow up and realise their masculine or feminine identities. Mothers are led to believe that it is inevitable and 'natural' that they should dedicate themselves to the care of their babies. The *agenda* is set so that 'good' mothering can only be viewed in the context of a 'good' mother being available continuously for *her* child. With this *agenda* the father is free to roam independent of *his* child. Significantly, the meanings of the words *her* and *his* are quite different. In their most savage forms, *her* means being confined, constrained and exhausted in parenting the child, and *his* means being isolated and alienated in breadwinning for the child.

The only chance to reset the *agenda* comes when the child reaches school age—then the state requires the 'good' mother to release her child for most of the child's waking day. The change in circumstances for the mother is enormous and, as recorded in previous chapters, it often brings with it a wish to work outside of the home. However, the 'good' mother is unable to reset the *agenda* so that she and the father share the responsibility for the child, rather the child remains almost entirely on her *agenda*. Children grow up to see that their mothers' identity and purpose in life is to serve and care for them; their fathers are seen to have an identity outside of the home in the 'important' breadwinning world.

Beginning preschool or school marks a significant change in the lives of young children. Their social world now has another focus which presents both complementary and conflicting experiences. At preschool children are tended almost solely by other women. As well as their female teachers, they interact with the mothers who attend the preschool for their allocated duty sessions. This provides another layer of legitimation to the children's developing view of a gender segregated world. The occasional father who performs a duty session is insufficient to alter this view. The key people in the preschool, the director and assistant, present a conflicting experience for the child. For, although they conform to the children's ideas of women serving and caring for them, they are also involved in this as paid work. The director is also manifestly in a position of authority in this new part of their world. Hence, unless their mothers are occupied in paid work, and in Tordale and Linfield this was rare with young children, preschool represents children's first regular encounter with women who work.

Primary school is a more complicated social world for children to understand than preschool, and it contains an even more complex web of conflicting and complementary experiences. Very often, even in a small school like Tordale, it is men who dominate and display the authority within the children's school world. Their own teacher is very likely to be a woman, but the principal, senior staff and those who enact discipline are likely to be men. However, the school does also present women of different ages and circumstances: some married, some parents, some single, some divorced, etc., all of whom have a tertiary education and are breadwinning. Hence, school provides a broader experience of significant women in the children's lives. In many respects, the difference between women teachers and pupils' mothers is greater than the difference between those teachers and their male colleagues. The distance between the women teachers and the Tordale and Linfield mothers is marked by the 'milestones' of education, career and money; the possession of each by the women teachers signifies some power, control or influence. The lesser difference between the men and women teachers stems from their commonality in these respects, in spite of their eventually diverging career paths. We shall see in this and the following chapter, that men and women teachers think and act as *teachers* in a way which is relatively undifferentiated in terms of their sex.

However, it is clear from Chapter 4 that the extent of gender division in the careers of teachers is enormous. This has substantial consequences for pupils because it helps form the production of the *gender agenda* in their lives. So, for example, when a teacher leaves school to have her baby and is not seen again by her pupils as a teacher, it marks a symmetrical shaping, between home and school, of the pupils' perceptions of gender. This symmetry is also marked by the men who control the school and wield their authority over the pupils' lives. The primary school is analogous to the family with the male staff as 'fathers'—having less contact, more power, authority and importance—and the female staff as 'mothers'—more contact, subordinate and of limited importance.

The family and the school are responsible for the production of the next generation. The changing conditions of society mean that both institutions are preparing this rising generation for a partly unknown future. In the Tordale and Linfield communities one sees such changing conditions emerging over the previous generation, for example, in the decline in farming and the rise of Blockie development. It is also possible to chart the broader social and economic changes which influence these communities, for example, the impact of 'new' technology, the internationalisation of finance and the increasing influence of women. Therefore, it is necessary when investigating the ways in which gender is being constructed in the young, to study, not only the reproduction of existing gender divisions, but also the ways in which gender is being incorporated into the future culture alongside other changes in communities and society.

In this last respect, school curricula represent a significant cultural statement of what is and what is expected to be. A school curriculum encapsulates heritage, contemporary context and future conditions. In a narrow and formal sense, curricula are statements about the sequential organisation, and the ways of teaching, selected knowledge, skills and values. These curricula are written and tangible; they can be pushed into an education system at several points to provide or be subjected to accountability, moderation, evaluation, assessment, verification or approval. In most societies these curricular statements are either formulated by a state authority for enactment by its schools or are developed by schools within guidelines laid down by the state. As instruments of the state, curricula reflect the values, biases, prejudices and divisions of society. And, through engagement with teachers and pupils, curricula reformulate those elements of society in the continuing construction of culture.

Teachers apply their own materials, skills, knowledge and interests when teaching a curriculum and pupils use their own knowledge, skills and interests to learn what is taught. Therefore, each curriculum becomes a unique product constructed in its classroom context. Its history can be traced back through the lives of the people involved and through the composition of the curriculum documents used by those people.

There is a sense in which everything experienced and learned at school becomes curriculum, either formal or hidden (Apple, 1971; 1979). Hence, seeing men in authority and women as child-care providers, becomes just as much a part of the school curriculum as do stories, songs, sums and sports. In fact, the entire school's operation as a social structure lays down its own *agendas* about the rules, values and conventions of the society in which it is located. Such *agendas* are not expressed as written statements, timetabled or assessed, however, as we shall see, they form a central part of school life and serve to produce and maintain the *gender agenda*.

* * *

The interviews with the Linfield and Tordale children provide a powerful insight into the foundation upon which they are building their adult lives. However, their explanations should be seen as ideas in flux. This is obvious when one considers that the six year old children we interviewed were only one-third of the way to commencing, in a legal sense at least, their adult lives; adult lives which run for several decades. The effect of age becomes evident in the different responses between the youngest and oldest children. Their views become more sophisticated and circumspect with age, suggesting that a continuing process is in train; a process in which gender is embedded but which is only partly shaped by the school. It is also shaped by the family, the community and the wider society through the mass-media (Edgar, 1980; Sampson, 1975).

In this chapter the relationship between the curricula at Tordale and Linfield, and the breadwinning, domestic and parenting *agendas*, is examined. The children's views about these aspects of adult life are discussed with reference to the ways curricula, family, community and mass-media affect them.

The breadwinning *agenda*

From their first day at school, the Linfield and Tordale pupils are exposed to an *agenda* about adult work. This rarely resides in the content of planned lessons and activities, but rather is expressed through the adults' school world. Part of the teacher-pupil relationship goes beyond the basic adult-child relationship into a worker/professional–client relationship. However, the term 'worker/professional–client' sits uneasily alongside the term 'teacher-pupil' because, even though calling teachers 'workers' or 'professionals' seems appropriate, calling pupils 'clients' does not. The Linfield and Tordale staff treat the parents as clients—not the pupils. But it is the pupils, not the parents, who engage the teachers as the basis of their paid work. This engagement amounts to a continuous, unfolding *agenda* about breadwinning. The children learn, largely through direct experience, about how teachers organise their breadwinning work.

Many of the principal attributes of paid work are lived out in the teachers' work at Linfield and Tordale. Elements such as routine, responsibility, punctuality, dress, manners, etc., are conveyed continuously alongside the occasional experiences of holidays, strikes, sick leave or maternity leave. The special morning tea break and gift collection for the staff member who is leaving are the accepted actions of workers. To the extent that the children are involved, they are learning how to be workers themselves. These experiences are enhanced by their understanding of other peoples' work: from family friends and relatives, through to their occasional encounters with other workers. The effect of gender on the working lives of the people they meet contributes to the setting of their own *gender agenda* about work. The symmetry between the gender relationships implicit in these experiences of breadwinning work and those at home concerning breadwinning, domestic and parenting labour, means that their embryonic *gender agenda* of work is based on a powerful, but false, premise.

Men matter

When I observe classes at Linfield I arrive about twenty minutes before school starts. Today is my third day of observing Marilyn Carmody's grade. She is one of those teachers who appears to be a natural; nothing seems to trouble her. Whatever her class of six year olds get up to, she exudes kindness, enthusiasm, humour and energy. My presence in her class is both welcomed and ignored: perfect. However, today Marilyn Carmody is late. Usually she is at school early to prepare busily for the arrival of her pupils. I wander off to the staffroom to see if she is there. Ted Symes, the principal, meets me as he is leaving the general office. 'Morning, Terry, how are things?' I could ask him if he knows where Marilyn Carmody is, but

I think better of it: researchers shouldn't 'dob' their subjects in for being late. 'Good thanks, how are things with you?' I receive a reply which suggests that Ted Symes wouldn't be first in the queue to join a Save Our Bureaucrats campaign, should someone declare an open season on the species.

In the staffroom a few teachers are having a caffeine-fix before confronting the working day. No sign of Marilyn Carmody and noone knows of her whereabouts. I am offered coffee, but I decline: a full bladder interferes with any researchers' observations. The electronic 'bell' pulses throughout the loudspeaker system; nothing reminds me more of my own school teaching. The rumble of massed footsteps in the corridors shows that the Linfield educational 'engine' has fired and is beginning to reach running temperature. As I leave the staffroom, James Porter comes to ask David Wilmets, who teaches in the next room to Marilyn Carmody, to keep an eye on her grade. Marilyn will be late because she has had a problem with her car. James and I walk to the classroom. He lets Marilyn Carmody's class into the room and tells them that she will be late. They are told to get their readers out and look at them until she arrives.

By the time Marilyn Carmody arrives the class are becoming quite restless. They greet her arrival with cheers and she immediately settles them down and apologises for being late. She describes her difficulties with her car and says that she had to telephone for an 'RACV man' to fix it. She manages skillfully to turn her earlier misfortune into a teaching topic and words such as 'battery' and 'jumper leads' are written on the blackboard. This is gradually turned into an introduction to a television programme the children are scheduled to see concerning people who work at sea.

In one corner of the room are neat rows of pictures of people doing different jobs. Marilyn Carmody is quite keen on the idea of equal opportunity between the sexes and has selected many of her curriculum materials on the basis of their inclusion of both sexes. So, in these pictures, we see women taxi drivers, police officers, carpenters and, more traditionally, nurses, but also doctors and veterinary surgeons. She wants her children to see women in jobs and careers as normal, and to see women in a wide variety of jobs.

Marilyn Carmody collects the television from David Wilmets' room and asks the children to sit on the mat in front of it. The programme lasts for fifteen minutes and covers some seafaring jobs in Britain, where the programme was made. Apart from one of the presenters, there are no women in the programme; we see lifeboatmen, lighthousemen, seamen, and fishermen. There is no time to talk about the programme at the end because it is recess. After recess we are off to the library where the teacher-librarian and Marilyn Carmody take up the matter of different jobs and show the children some related books. Some of the books represent the 'new wave' which are inclusive of both sexes, but most of the library's stocks, including those about the sea, have not been washed with the 'new wave'.

Later in the day Marilyn Carmody and a few children discuss wild animals. There are many animals presented from a series of pictures, ranging from koalas through to the big cats and elephants of Africa and Asia. Listening to the discussion with the critical ear of a researcher I notice that the only time that the female of the species is mentioned is when either the picture or the topic make it absolutely necessary. Otherwise all the animals are referred to as males, even though, presumably, half are females.

During the afternoon Marilyn Carmody decides that they will sing some songs. The children love singing with their teacher. She takes out her guitar and adeptly strums the first few chords of some songs and the children follow her. Marilyn Carmody becomes the entertainer; her years of amateur folk singing have left her with a repertoire and style which captivates the children. Small percussion instruments are distributed and the children produce an enthusiastic cacophony of bangs, tinkles and chimes. In the confines of the classroom my ears are subjected to a piercing, discordant noise; occasionally, Marilyn Carmody's voice and playing rises above the noise and the children fall in to her rhythm and pitch, only to drift off again into noise. The instruments are packed away and the singing session concludes with requests from the children. Several shout out their choice and I form the impression that Marilyn Carmody is selecting songs she feels are appropriate: mostly quiet ones. However, each time Marilyn Carmody asks for requests there is an increasing number of children requesting the same song: one which she ignores conspicuously. Then, without announcement, she plays the first bars of this, their last, song. The children smile excitedly: this is the best song she has ever taught them. The song: 'She wore an itsy bitsy, teeny weeny, yellow, polka dot bikini'; they call it, 'the bikini song'.

What can we understand about the breadwinning *agenda* from this description of some events in Marilyn Carmody's day? James Porter's arrangements for someone to cover her lateness to work, Marilyn Carmody's explanation to her class and even my reluctance to ask the Principal if he knew of her whereabouts, all say something about the way adults accept the significance of punctuality and responsibility to others in their breadwinning work. The children see James Porter working as a person (man) in authority as deputy principal. Another teacher's work is temporarily extended to assume some of Marilyn Carmody's responsibility for her class. On arrival she uses the circumstances for her lateness as the core of a class discussion during which the work of a motor mechanic is presented as being important and useful. This work is only discussed in terms of the mechanic being male.

We know that Marilyn Carmody favours equality between the sexes and that, when she consciously selected curriculum materials and activities, she endeavoured to be inclusive of both sexes. However, her discussion with the class after her late arrival illustrates the hidden assumptions about gender of even those who have a level of critical awareness about the matter. Without hesitation she presents the traditional view of cars and mechanical things as being men's work. Her own limitation in these areas surfaces in her inability to diagnose and remedy her car's fault and in her difficulty in describing the event to the the children. This raises the question of the relative effect on children of 'new wave' curriculum materials, books, sports and activities, when set against the tide of life examples provided by significant adults.

In addition, Marilyn Carmody's curriculum includes selections from the broadcast media over which she has no control. In the example presented, the international nature of gender divisions in the workplace is evident. The maritime work in the television programme is replete with images of strength, toughness, bravery and excitement; there are no 'new waves' of sexual equality in these seascapes. She tunes in to a global legitimation of what she is teaching: men's work matters. The visit to the library reflects a similar pattern: for every book such as one entitled, 'Emily the Engine Driver', there are numerous others fitting neatly with the traditional gender structures of work. Even stories about animals or imaginary characters are vested with the cultural limitations of gender, as if they too were members of the human race.

The singing session presents her as the competent singer and guitarist. Most of the songs have roots in the traditional culture formed by adults for children, their *agenda* includes: violence, sexism, militarism, royalism, humour, fantasy, sadness and compassion. A few songs are more contemporary and come from the adult world, especially of popular folk music. But the 'bikini song' has its roots much more firmly embedded in the pop music world which emerged some thirty years ago. It seems to symbolise the move these children will make from children's songs to an adolescent pop culture: a culture of image and sexuality. Television, which is legitimated at school as a 'good' medium, peddles its pop videos and songs to eager eyes and ears. Pop video programmes such as 'Countdown'—which, amongst other things, broadcast its pop consumerism throughout Australia for more than a decade—leave them with a more gender malleable, but still sexist and sexual, view of work. In this case, work is in the pop music industry, an industry which is highly exploitative, especially of women (Steward and Garratt, 1984).

Children are introduced to the world of breadwinning in direct ways. The school's curricula include excursions to see people at work. Miriam Tate took her prep grade to a local fish shop, other children in the school visit workplaces such as a fire station, power station or farm. Sometimes people attend the school to talk about their jobs, for example, a potter, police officer or mechanic; occasionally these people are parents from the school community. At other times people come to school to do their work, such as a health visitor, psychologist or plumber. Because each of these encounters with breadwinning occurs in the schools' communities they directly reflect the gender differentiation which exists in those communities. So, when schools include such encounters as part of the curriculum, children are not only experiencing particular types of work and workplaces, but also the ways gender shapes such work and workplaces.

The relationship between work and education is made explicit by teachers and other adults who visit Tordale and Linfield schools. Sometimes this is expressed simply as the children needing to *work* hard at school in order to achieve particular occupations. On other occasions, it is expressed specifically in terms of particular subjects needing to be studied. For example, Donna Morton discussed the work of a National Park ranger, a job that she aspired to as a school child, with a group of Tordale children. She advised the children that they needed to pass their Higher School Certificate and study maths and science subjects. Some weeks later, in their interviews, two grade four children said they would like to be National Park rangers. However, none of the Linfield children mentioned this occupation. In the absence of a detailed longitudinal study, it is difficult to assess the effect of teachers' actions and statements on the lives of children. However, this case at Tordale does show that there is some degree of endurance.

The pupils' explanations of the jobs they would like to do in adult life show remarkable conformity with the gender and class composition of their communities. However, the children's ages are also important. Their sophistication and understanding of the world of work increases with age, with some of the youngest finding it difficult even to think of themselves as being paid workers. Some young children said they would play on their BMX bike or make 'cubby' houses as adults, however, most gave a single simple job, for example, nurse or shop assistant. At Linfield the jobs specified by the prep through to grade two children were less varied, and more often working class, than those specified by the fewer similar aged children at Tordale. The younger Tordale children gave occupations including: doctor, teacher, Lego maker and spaceman. In all, 56 children were interviewed at Linfield and 28 at Tordale. One might have expected that with the substantial exposure to teaching as an occupation the children would have nominated this job relatively frequently, but no child at Linfield and only two at Tordale nominated school teaching. A further two Tordale children said they would like piano or gymnastics teaching.

The social class composition of the Tordale and Linfield communities is reflected by the occupations the children nominated. Apart from archetypal fantasy occupations such as movie star or astronaut, the Linfield children generally confined their occupations to trades, services such as police, ambulance or army, or shop, office and banking work. A few Linfield children opted to be doctors, architects or vets. At Tordale the children cast their net further. Jobs such as: pilot, choreographer, scientist, author and professor were included alongside those of doctor, vet, nurse, park ranger and farmer. Some Tordale children chose traditional working-class occupations in the trade and semi-skilled areas, such as plumber, carpenter, bulldozer driver or typist. In contrast with Linfield children, none of them mentioned working as shop assistants, but in concert with Linfield, there were some who wanted to join the police force.

An analysis of the children's choices of occupation shows that there are some clear links with the occupations of their parents and, occasionally, siblings. For example, at Tordale, Jacqueline wants to be a doctor like her father and Lily wants to be a typist like her sister. At Linfield, Brett wants to follow his father as an ambulance officer and Mary says she 'would like to be a hairdresser like my Mum' (Linfield, grade two). Without exception, all the children who opted for a trade or semi-skilled job came from families where these occupations are their way of breadwinning. Although the children who nominated middle-class occupations were often from middle-class families, there were also some who came from working-class backgrounds. Several chosen occupations would need to be treated with circumspection, for example, the fantasy occupations of astronaut or film star, and the fragile careers in soccer or motorcross. It seems probable that the children—mostly boys—who specify these occupations in primary school will change them for something more commonplace before they leave school. One expects that most children change their views about the job they aspire to during their schooling, however, their changes are likely to remain consistent with the labour market and with their class and gender positions.

The links are solid between gender and the children's nominated occupations. No boy nominated a job seen as traditionally female and only one girl nominated a traditional male job; Christine (grade six, Linfield) wanted to be a truck driver like her father, but she thought her mother would be opposed to this. The jobs selected only by girls include: doctor, vet, nurse, hairdresser, teacher, typist and film star; those selected only by boys include: farmer, carpenter, plumber, soccer player, astronaut and mechanic. There are some jobs which were given by both sexes, for example, National Park ranger, artist and police officer (more popular with boys). Each of the above jobs was specified by two or more children. The girls' choices include more jobs where the educational level, status and rewards are higher: doctor, nurse, teacher and vet. They are attracted to these jobs because of the working relationships: with people in general, children or animals. Material gain is of more interest to boys than girls, however, this is usually expressed in terms of having a nice house, cars etc., rather than in terms of being especially wealthy. Some of the girls have interests in owning a nice house and furnishings. The overall impression is that the children are not concerned with the breadwinning nature of occupations, but with the type of everyday activities involved.

A few of the girls gave occupations accompanied by saying that they would be a housewife. Cheryl had given the idea some thought: 'I was asking Mum the other day would the housewife be the easiest job and she said "no". You have to be a Mum and a wife and a cleaner and a vacuum cleaner' (grade three, Tordale). In thinking about their adult lives, there is a close relationship between girls and their mothers. This can be attributed partly to the girls' attempts to understand what it is to be women, and partly to the disproportionate amount of parenting labour performed by mothers. The boys recognise that their adult lives will be outside of the home, but they have little experience, unless they live on a farm, of what this might entail. The girls have a similar recognition in relation to breadwinning work, but the lure of domestic and parenting labour is strong. Hence, the gender differentiated breadwinning ambitions for the children are interwoven with an unfolding understanding of their other future adult roles. The conformity to traditional gender positions is substantial, although the older children show some flexibility and even questioning of such traditions.

The children were asked what they thought about men and women pursuing non-traditional jobs. The younger children were given examples such as men nurses or kindergarten teachers or women plumbers, pilots or truck drivers. The response from John (prep, Tordale) was instantaneous: 'Yukky'. The two girls in his interview group were more reserved. Lana said: 'A bit strange to me because I haven't seen one.' Lily agreed: 'It sounds a bit strange to me, a girl bus driver and a girl plumber. I haven't seen one. I've only seen a man bus driver and a man plumber'. Her use of the term 'girl' for women is perhaps indicative of a process which portrays women as weak and incapable: like children. In most cases, it is the boys who oppose crossing gender barriers in the workplace. David (grade two, Linfield,) explained: 'I reckon that if girls want to work in hospitals they'd be a nurse and not a doctor. I reckon boys should be the doctor'. Mary disagreed, 'I think if a man is a nurse and a girl a doctor, I think that's fair. Then if you want to be a doctor and you're a girl and you can't be a doctor, then it wouldn't be fair'. James entered the debate with an observation from a television programme: 'I watch Country Practice. . . Vicki is a vet, Brendan is a nurse and Simon is a doctor'.

Television is an important window on the world of work for children and, at the touch of a button, its images of gender can provide them with wide horizons or narrow vistas. Depending on its content, television entertainment can be enslavement or enrichment. Women in non-traditional jobs are acceptable to the children if they have either experienced it or seen it on television. Otherwise their opinions range from being dismissive of women's abilities through to being fiercely sexist. Tanya (grade three, Linfield) believes that women would not be very good at panel beating, which is her father's occupation, 'The men would have to go over it again. The women might scratch it and not paint it properly. They probably could do it, but the men could do it better'. Leila agreed with Tanya and provided another example, 'If a girl came and did building with the boys she would be crazy. It's a man's job. Girls can't lift fifteen bricks at once, boys could'. Andrew added, 'I don't think girls can chop down trees'. These grade three children at Linfield, perhaps because of the working class nature of the community, see only examples of women's incapability or unsuitability for manual skills and labour. They give no explanation of why women are incapable of such work or, conversely, why men are capable. Their rationale rests on what is, apparently, 'natural' or 'common sense'.

There is a watershed in opinion between grades three and four. By grade four the children, especially the girls, had begun to question the assumptions of the past and to espouse egalitarian views. At Tordale, the grade four children neatly exemplify this watershed. Jason observed that he thought women bus drivers would attract more men passengers, but that women electricians 'would blow the place up'. Damien argued that 'women aren't built the right way... they can't do the things that we are (sic)'. Then Ruth retorted, 'You can't have a baby or anything...I can do anything a man can do'. This led to an argument between the two boys and two girls in the group. One Tordale boy was concerned as to who would do the domestic labour if women are in the paid workforce. This problem had not escaped the Linfield boys either, as this exchange in a grade five interview shows.

> I reckon women should stick to the housework...So the Dads get the money and the women don't have to get the money. They can just stay at home and get the Dad's money. (Carl)
>
> I think if you're not married you're free to do anything you like, you can go and do anything...If they're married they could too...If the children were about three it would be pretty stupid (Kathy)
>
> I think there should be equal rights...they can do what they want (Lynette)
>
> I'm with Carl because I reckon that men should go out and work and that women should clean up the house. Because women, if they work in a motel, they can burn themselves and all that. (William)

The grade five children at Tordale are in favour of people being able to choose non-traditional work:

> I think it would be all right if you're really happy to do that job, if you're a girl. (Claire)
>
> I reckon it's good. Some people reckon it's bad, but I think it's good. (Matthew)
>
> They should be independent. (Peter)
>
> Ladies, they don't have a good wide choice of jobs as men do. (Matthew)
>
> Some people think boys are better than girls...I think boys and girls are just the same...in value. (Claire)
>
> Some jobs ladies can do that men can't do, for example, some men can't cook. (Matthew)
>
> I think ladies should be able to do it. If men, they're sick, then the lady might have to take over for a few days. (Peter)

The children's emphases are on women doing non-traditional jobs, rather than men. Because women are encouraged to pursue so few occupations, reducing gender barriers to jobs means providing access to the large pool of 'men's' work. This provides a wider choice to women and, thereby, to primary school girls.

The gender barriers to men pursuing the few traditional 'women's jobs' are quite rigid. A man who becomes, for example, a kindergarten teacher or nurse, endures sexist and pernicious comments from others outside of his work. However, a woman who becomes, for example, an engineer or surveyor endures similar resistance from her colleagues in addition to others outside of her work. There are now some areas of 'men's' work where women's representation is sufficient for them to be an accepted minority, for example, in medicine, dentistry or gardening. This acceptance has not reduced men's domination over these occupations, but it gives women a foothold from which future generations can move forward.

A major problem for those who cross the gender barrier to work is the questions this raises about their sexuality, masculinity or femininity. Jane (grade six, Linfield) made the point: 'I don't think much of it (non-traditional work) because I have always wanted what every woman does, and not a man'. There are three types of response to the idea of non-traditional work from the older children. Some girls such as Jane, are concerned that work on the other side of the gender barrier is threatening to their femininity. Boys do not express similar concerns because none actively considers non-traditional work. Some boys give a different type of response, typified by Steven (grade six, Tordale) who said, in reference to women doing non-traditional work: 'As long as they know what they are doing you can't really stop them'. Such boys are not awash with egalitarian values, but are drifting with the tide. Clearly, they are not happy with women pursuing jobs which they see as 'theirs'. But they are not going to initiate any resistance alone. For some of these boys their concerns spread to domestic labour. They understand that if women participate in breadwinning then more domestic labour is destined for them.

The third, and most common response, comes from boys and girls. Simply, they believe people should be able to do any job they wish. Christine (grade six, Linfield) received agreement from her interview group when she declared, regarding being able to do non-traditional work, 'It's good because it gives you a chance to be something that you really want to be'. These children are not saying that they want to cross the gender barrier. Rather they are declaring two things: they want all jobs to be open to them and they are happy for others to avail themselves of such opportunities. It is worth remembering that one's occupation forms a considerable part of one's personal identity. These children recognise that 'to be something you really want to be' means breadwinning in a chosen way. The extent to which these children are able to choose their jobs, depends not only on the options available to them in the labour market, but also on the limitations they impose on themselves in response to the prevailing social structural conditions. These conditions are reflected in the curriculum and are perpetuated through its processes and forms, some of which we have seen to be contradictory.

The domestic *agenda*

The domestic *agenda* plays a smaller part in the schools' worlds than does the breadwinning *agenda*. Thinking, talking and learning about people's work are often important features of school curricula, but there is little consideration of routine domestic labour. However, teachers bring elements of domestic labour into focus through occasional classroom and outside episodes. Frequently, such episodes serve to present women—the children's mothers—as the only domestic labourers. Miriam Tate represents a typical case from Linfield. She refers to matters of domestic labour as solely the responsibility and preserve of women, even though she believes in, and to some extent lives, a more egalitarian life herself. Some examples may serve to make this clear. One morning the children were given plasticene to work with. Miriam Tate told the children to 'knead it like your mother does when she makes scones'. On the following afternoon the children were set a task using small plastic counters. They were told to place them in a stack about which she commented, 'Sometimes when your mother makes pancakes, she makes a stack of them'. On another occasion the children were told to ask their mothers to pack their school lunches in a small paper or plastic bag so that these could be used to collect leaves in after lunch.

Each of these small episodes is harmless and innocuous. However, when aggregated with many other examples, Miriam Tate's prep grade children receive a subtle, sometimes hidden, *agenda* of domestic labour. This *agenda* reflects, and is beginning to reproduce, the traditional gender divided domestic labour of the home. The taken-for-granted nature of these episodes implies that such gender division is seen by the teacher and the school as 'natural' and unproblematic. However, they are clearly at the root of sexual differences in society.

To a lesser extent, fathers are mentioned in connection with the forms of labour they perform around the home. Here again, the various maintenance and repair jobs are referred to as fathers' work as if this is the only possibility. All teachers spoke in these ways, even those who are sometimes deliberately inclusive of both sexes. We asked some of the teachers about such examples and none of them saw them as significant. Some could not remember even saying them.

The 'new wave' curricula which provide for breadwinning to be presented in non-sexist ways do not have similar provision for domestic labour. Domestic labour is relatively ignored, remains unimportant and rests at women's feet. The equivalent of domestic labour in the school classroom—the various chores and tasks which form part of classroom life such as cleaning blackboards, emptying waste paper bins, collecting equipment etc.—is often shared between the sexes. Teachers such as Miriam Tate and Donna Morton, and Rod Miles the Tordale principal, try to allocate tasks equally amongst their pupils. They aim to allocate manual tasks such as carrying bins or lifting chairs to all children, however, some of their colleagues are more inclined to allocate these tasks to boys. In particular, Mary Thomson and Stephanie Bell, who are amongst the oldest and most experienced teachers, maintain the most discriminatory practices. They aim to impart chivalry as a form of courteous social behaviour, part of which includes boys performing the majority of the manual tasks.

Most children spend a few days at a school camp during their primary schooling. Usually, these are held in permanent camp buildings operated by schools, outdoor education organisations or holiday companies. Some children, usually the older grades, camp in tents. Such breaks from home life provide the opportunity for an alternative view of domestic labour. However, our observation records from Linfield and Tordale camps show that domestic labour is not organised very differently.

Linfield's grade five visited a Ministry of Education camp about 120 kilometres from the school. It was located in an old gold mining town in the Great Dividing Range. One female and two male teachers took 27 children to the camp for a school week in November. Two mothers were invited to join the camp and, apart from general supervision of the children, their main task was to prepare the meals. They had worked at school camps in the previous two years when their children first attended. It was a source of enjoyment to them because they liked being with the children, appreciated the countryside and welcomed the break from home.

Tordale's camp was held in a secondary school's lakeside camp about 70 kilometres from the school. The principal's wife, Rebecca

Miles, came to the camp as the cook. Rod Miles and Carmel Walls were the teachers. All parents were invited to visit the camp whenever they liked and when we attended there were three mothers there for the day. These mothers helped in the kitchen and participated in the activities with the children.

At each camp some forms of domestic labour were regimented and performed by the children. Setting tables, washing dishes and some food preparation were allocated to groups of children. Each group was also responsible for cleaning and tidying its room. At the Tordale camp, Rod Miles organised morning inspections with the children lined-up outside their rooms. Such things were more informal at the Linfield camp. Laundry was usually stored and taken home (for Mum!)

School camps have *agendas* that intersect with those of the school. but which enter new territory for the children. The new territory includes the natural environment of the camps, bushcraft and outdoor education. Also the children experienced being away from home and living with their peers and teachers. Both school camps required the participation of all children in the activities. So, boys and girls had opportunities to try new things for themselves, although the nature of participation varied. School camps are a context in which domestic labour comes into the curriculum in a formal and practical way. Teachers and mothers showed the children how to perform the various tasks and set the rules for this work. However, given that it was women who were responsible for the domestic labour in the camp kitchens, the traditional gender division of domestic labour was replicated by the school.

The division between the teachers and the mothers was quite clear. The teachers were the 'bosses' who gave the orders to the children and were served by the mothers. Rebecca Miles occupied a position 'senior' to the other mothers who attended the camp, she also was more direct in giving orders to the children, especially in the kitchen and dining area. At the Tordale camp a father arrived for a couple of hours during lunchtime. He spent most of the time talking to the teachers and mothers, and, apart from helping to cook on the barbecue—arguably the only traditional context in which Australian men cook—he left the domestic labour to the mothers. Along with their male colleagues, the women teachers also left the domestic labour to the mothers. This demonstrates the distance between the women teachers and the children's mothers which was discussed in the previous two chapters.

School camps also offer the opportunity for teachers and pupils to understand each other in a more personal way. Relationships are less formal than those that occur in the classroom. Dave Stone, a younger teacher at Linfield, played upon heterosexuality in his relationships with the girls at the camp. He frequently used terms such as 'gorgeous', 'beautiful' and 'darling' when teaching the girls. Mostly the girls appreciated these references and he seemed to enjoy being the focus of female attention. Such exchanges serve to construct the importance of masculinity and femininity to the children; they are also a foundation for, and an expectation of, future heterosexuality.

Heterosexuality creeps into school *agendas* in other subtle ways. Mary Thomson, an older teacher at Linfield and one of the most traditionally sexist in her teaching, follows a procedure for allowing visiting children to enter her class. When a child knocks on her classroom door during a lesson, usually to bring a message from another teacher, the child is greeted with the words, 'Come in if you're good looking'. The child slides back the door to be confronted by the children and teacher gazing at him or her. Mary Thomson then asks the class, 'Is he/she good looking?' The class respond with mixed yells of 'yes' and 'no'. Some visiting children, when exposed to this attention to their physical attributes, looked as if they wished they could melt away. Others played the part and would flaunt themselves to the class.

Mary Thomson's and Dave Stone's behaviour can be construed as harmless fun, helping to generate a friendly relationship with their pupils. However, it is predicated on romantic, heterosexual relationships; relationships which are the foundation of traditional Western family formation and which lead to the deep gender divisions of adult life (Delamont, 1980b:71-94). Such fragments of primary school *agendas* mesh with the powerful sexual messages and images of the mass media to imprison children inside a socially constructed model of 'normal' adult life. Religion acts as one jailer and the state another. The wedding ceremony formalises and legalises this normality and the processes of human and social reproduction almost inevitably follow. Marriage usually marks an official change in a man's domestic servant; his mother is replaced by his wife.

The previous chapter described how the Linfield and Tordale children are developing their understanding of domestic labour. Although some of them, especially the older ones, showed signs of a readiness to share domestic labour in adult life, the prevailing view followed traditional gender segregated lines. At the extreme, some boys rejected having to perform domestic labour, although no girls made such a rejection. Presumably, unless these boys change their views, they will need to ensure that throughout their lives they have a women to work for them.

'New wave' curricula in schools provide non-sexist approaches within the usual range of curricular activities. However, we can see that a curriculum of domestic labour in schools is meagre. Schools are often enjoined by business and employer organisations to prepare children for breadwinning work, but domestic work, formally ignored at school, is informally delineated as women's work. The hidden agenda of domestic labour at Linfield and Tordale reinforces the traditional gender divisions; there is no challenge to the traditional organisation of this everyday work.

The parenting *agenda*

The work the Linfield and Tordale mothers do at school camps is seen by them as parenting work. It is part of being 'good' parents, in much the same way as working in the Linfield school canteen (which makes a good profit) or providing hot soup on winter lunchtimes at Tordale, is being a 'good' parent. Yet schools exploit mothers in a way that they are unable to do with fathers. They do this by feeding upon the traditional gender divisions in the community which restrict women's breadwinning opportunities and load the bulk of domestic and parenting labour upon them. It would be difficult for Linfield and Tordale schools to operate as cheaply and smoothly without the labour provided by their 'reserve armies' of mothers.

Fathers are also asked to provide labour for the schools. This labour takes the form of occasional mowing, repair, maintenance and construction work: 'men's' work. Hence, the children see parents working at their school in forms of labour which mirror the traditional gender segregation of the community. The *agenda* is that 'good' parents help their children by working for schools in these ways.

Much of the parenting *agenda* at Tordale and Linfield operates in hidden forms. Those women teachers who leave when pregnant and are not seen again as teachers in the school pass on a powerful message to their pupils about their exclusive responsibilities, as mothers, for their children. Those men teachers who, ignoring family leave provisions, continue their careers instead of taking responsibility for their children, provide further testimony to this.

Of course, this is not something unique to teaching. The organisation of breadwinning work typically ignores or excludes the parenting responsibilities of the workforce. Indeed, historically, men's work conditions and wage levels are set on the basis that they are free to work without the encumbrance of parenting responsibilities, but that they need to support families. In effect, this means supporting their womenfolk to do the parenting for them.

Today, women's participation in the workforce is increasing. In 1947, 25 per cent of women were in the workforce, by 1986 it was 49 per cent. For married women over the same period the increase is from 7 per cent to 46 per cent (Wajcman and Rosewarne, 1986:15-17). The small changes to childcare provision in the workplace and the large increase in community childcare have been brought about by women. Although a few men also use these services, it is the presence of women in the workforce which has stimulated this change, not the presence of 'new wave' fathers demanding childcare for their children. Once children reach school age, schools provide an important childcare service for breadwinning parents.

At school, the hidden *agenda* of parenting intrudes into the organisation of school and classroom activities. Newsletters to parents at Linfield are consistently non-sexist in their language, although there are some items directed to mothers. Often, the source of these items is the parents' club. Jane Peters, as parents' club president, regularly included matters in the school's newsletter relating to events or activities that fathers often avoid, for example, chocolate making or cake decoration demonstrations. Tordale, being a small school, uses many informal networks to communicate with parents. As the only parents' group was the mothers' club (which has latterly become a parents' club) it was an instrument for excluding fathers from some parenting responsibilities and discussion in the community. The presence and activities of the mothers' club formed part of Tordale's parenting *agenda*. However, these mothers presented a view of 'mothers' as more assertive and powerful than was the case at Linfield. It was this assertiveness and power Rod Miles sought to circumscribe because it challenged his power as principal.

Within the classroom, the parenting *agenda* continues on traditional gender segregated lines. Even women who are sensitive to sexism fall into the trap of assuming that some forms of parenting are only performed by mothers. Miriam Tate is a case in point. Her biography and career have been described previously. She is a woman who actively resists sexist elements in her work. We saw earlier that she usually saw domestic labour as a woman's work and this extended to parenting. For example, she often said to the children at the end of the school day 'if your Mum's here, you may go'. On one such occasion there were three fathers and one mother outside the classroom, although more mothers arrived soon after. The message is that it is mothers' responsibility to collect their children from school; if fathers collect their children, presumably, this is their choice or an exception, but not their responsibility.

Some parts of the school curriculum transmit 'hidden' messages to the children about parenthood, in particular, or 'appropriate' concepts of masculinity and femininity, in general. Children's stories, apart from some of the 'new wave' ones, portray mothers as responsible for child care. Even stories about the bird, animal and insect worlds vest them with a 'human' gender order and install them in nuclear families.

Government policy requires the primary school sports curriculum to include both sexes, but the reality is that the gender-structured nature of sport in contemporary culture passes on to children. Men's 'major' sport dominates the mass media throughout the world; in Victoria, the Victorian Football League (VFL) is the bloated patriarch which gorges itself on the lion's share of media coverage. The male hegemony of the VFL extends into the primary school where its symbols abound and monuments are erected to its honour. In spite of government policy, the inclusion of girls in playing Australian rules football at school only serves to remind them that they are excluded from participation in the VFL.

Some football players and other male 'heroes' are incorporated into contemporary culture and transformed, through the mass media, into images of masculinity and heterosexual attraction. Children at Linfield and Tordale have the names of these men etched on their bags, rulers, clothes and, one assumes, minds. The schools help to legitimise these masculine images in their recognition of them as occasional significant topics for discussion and work in class. Beneath these images of popular men lies an *agenda* of male hegemony and romantic heterosexual attachment; two elements which drive the formation of new, gender segregated, families.

We have seen that the children of Linfield and Tordale are forming their views about adult life and are wrestling with the ideas of masculinity and femininity presented to them. The majority of the children, especially the younger ones, said that they would marry and have children. Some of the older children were either uncertain or said that they would not marry. The older girls were more likely than the boys to express uncertainty or rejection of marriage; for boys to reject marriage would leave them without domestic labour. Girls were also more likely to question whether they would have children, as Kathy (grade six, Linfield) said, 'I'm not keen on the idea...because they're too much trouble'. Such girls understand parenting as their responsibility and they are unsure if this is what they want. Some of them are concerned about child bearing. Maureen (grade one, Linfield) said, 'I don't want to have a baby because it will hurt me'.

Perhaps, if the Linfield and Tordale school curricula had approached parenting as a problematic issue, they might have found that there is interest amongst the pupils in discussing this aspect of their future lives. As it is, the parenting *agenda* remains hidden and, along with its domestic and breadwinning counterparts, serves only to nudge the children gently along the road to traditional, gender-divided adult lives.

7 Classroom life

As we have seen, a curriculum ranges over all the activities of the school, but is most intensely focused on the school classroom. It is here that the children's world of schooling is constructed and lived out through a complexity of experiences and actions. Most children spend over 1000 hours each year in their primary school classrooms working through the curriculum.

The school's *agendas* of classroom life are dynamic entities that are continuously melded, modified and manipulated by the people involved. Children and teachers contribute to the curriculum and to classroom life by bringing their own life and media experiences to bear. They use their imagination and creativity to mix everchanging curriculum 'cocktails' which are learned and lived in the classroom. While those who create formal curriculum programmes may assume them to be fixed and firm, pupils and teachers pick and choose, reorder and reorganise, add and subtract to make their own particular curriculum 'cocktails'.

The power of individuals in the classroom to influence the direction and use of the curriculum is not equal. Typically, teachers are the most powerful people and make many curriculum decisions before the pupils become involved. Thereafter, a variety of individual and collective elements interact to construct everyday curricular experiences. Gender affects the interaction processes of the classroom in several ways. My previous research in preschools and primary schools shows that girls' imagination and creativity is less recognised and rewarded than the boys' and also that boys receive more attention than girls from their teachers (Evans, 1979; 1980; 1982a; 1984c). Leder (1986) has also demonstrated this latter point in recent research in primary schools.

Studies in secondary schools show that teachers continue to discriminate in favour of boys and maintain the subservient position of girls throughout their school lives (for example, Cosgrove, 1981; Sampson, 1979; Spender, 1982; Taylor, 1980, 1982). We have seen in the previous chapter how teachers apply the adult *gender agenda* to both the formal and informal aspects of schooling. Clarricoates's (1978) research in British primary schools also shows how teachers, often unconsciously, organise classroom life towards the maintenance of male hegemony.

It is usual to assume, as is the case in the research evidence just cited, that teachers are paramount in shaping the events of classroom life. Therefore, classroom interaction research primarily focuses on what teachers do or say in their classrooms (e.g. Delamont, 1976; Flanders, 1970). As any teacher knows, there are times when they feel anything but paramount in their classrooms. Indeed, some research has studied the ways students assert themselves or create their own meanings and actions in the school or classroom (e.g. Davies, 1984; Hargreaves, Hester and Mellor, 1975; Willis, 1977). Brophy and Good argue that teachers are 'primarily reactive rather than proactive' in their interactions with students (1974: 229). The vicissitudes of classroom life allow pupils either to submit to or to subvert their teachers. The social control aspects of teaching are often seen as the yardstick of being a good teacher, but, in essence, most of the social control measures used by teachers are used in response to pupil actions.

Clarricoates (1978) and Levy (1974) have shown not only that teachers deem control and discipline to be of major importance to their work, but also that girls are less likely than boys to challenge their control. James Porter, the Linfield deputy principal, recognised this and suggested that primary school is 'girl orientated' because 'there are a lot of expectations such as neatness, quietness, which girls fit into and boys less so'. He also argues that the 'ocker' form of masculinity which some boys adopt includes verbal and physical aggression which schools discourage.

The fact that teachers are concerned about maintaining discipline and control and try to impose relatively quiet and passive forms of behaviour suggests the power of pupils to affect school and classroom life. The increasingly common tales of teacher stress, littered with anecdotes about disruptive children, support this conclusion. In short, children have an important and fundamental effect on the course of classroom life, and on the lives of teachers.

For these reasons, it was decided to record interactions between teachers and pupils, and who initiated them. During our week's observation in each classroom, we recorded each interaction between classroom teacher and pupils. We only recorded interactions having a verbal component, thus, purely non-verbal interactions were not recorded as interactions, although the meaning and context may have been recorded as part of the qualitative record of events. This qualitative record, in the form of written notes, also contains descriptions of some of the more substantial verbal interactions. Within the scope of one observer, this provides a very detailed record of the numbers and initiators of interactions, together with a qualitative record of what took place. Specific events were followed up in informal discussions with the teachers during breaks from teaching.

Interactions—the figures

In all, eight classrooms were observed for a week: six at Linfield and two at Tordale. Carmel Walls's class at Tordale—a composite prep, one and two grade—also had Donna Morton as a teacher in the mornings, increasing the possibility of interactions between a teacher and pupils. The other classes were the sole responsibility of one teacher and, although they were occasionally taken by other teachers, only the interactions with the classroom teacher were recorded. Interactions with Donna Morton were included because she spent over half the teaching time each day with the class.

In the following tables, the basic figure presented is the mean (average) interaction score per day for boys or girls. This figure is calculated by adding all the interactions relating to boys or girls and then dividing by the number of boys or girls in attendance on that day. In this way differences in the numbers of boys and girls in the classes and in the attendances each day are accommodated. The figures in brackets throughout are percentages of the total interactions to the nearest whole number.

In Table 7.1 the overall figures for Linfield and Tordale are presented. These represent a very broad picture of the interactions at the two schools because they represent a total of thirty days of observation at Linfield and ten days at Tordale. Each column shows the mean number of interactions per day followed by the percentage of the total of the particular interaction type. For example, each girl observed at Linfield initiated an average of 2.9 interactions each day with her teacher. This represents 53 per cent of all the pupil initiated interactions. Likewise, each Tordale boy was involved in an average of 12.3 interactions with his teacher, which represents 58 per cent of teacher initiated interactions.

Table 7.1 Mean daily teacher and pupil initiated interaction scores at Linfield and Tordale

	Teacher initiated interactions		Pupil initiated interactions		All interactions	
	male recipient	female recipient	male	female	male	female
Linfield: mean per day	6.8 (56%)	5.3 (44%)	2.6 (47%)	2.9 (53%)	9.4 (53%)	8.2 (47%)
Tordale: mean per day	12.3 (58%)	8.9 (42%)	4.6 (44%)	5.9 (56%)	16.9 (53%)	14.8 (47%)

The greater number of interactions per pupil recorded at Tordale occurred because the teacher-pupil ratio is less than at Linfield. Tordale has to cater for a similar range of ages and subjects to Linfield, but has a much smaller school population than Linfield. The class sizes at Tordale were in the low twenties and those at Linfield were about 30. In addition, as was stated previously, Carmel Walls's class often had Donna Morton teaching as well. However, when the percentages of all interactions are considered we find that these two schools have precisely the same proportion of interactions involving the same sex. In both cases, boys have a slightly greater proportion (53%) of interactions with their teachers than the girls (47%).

The relative equality of these percentages is brought about by summing the teacher initiated and pupil initiated columns: columns which show figures of quite different complexions. In these columns, the Tordale boys received 58 per cent of the teacher initiated interactions and the Linfield boys received 56 per cent: an average of 57 per cent across the two schools. However, the girls initiated more interactions with their teachers, 56 per cent at Tordale and 53 per cent at Linfield. The fact that the girls initiated more interactions with their teachers than did the boys runs counter to most other research. In a study of primary school mathematics and language lessons, Leder (1986) found that boys contributed the only statistically significant differences in pupil initiated interactions. More broadly, Spender states that, 'girls don't talk as much as boys in mixed classrooms. . . These facts. . . have been provided in numerous research findings' (1980:148). Elliott (1974), in a case-history of his teaching of an innovative secondary school curriculum during 1970 in Britain, demonstrates Spender's point. However, Davies (1984) cites British research by Fuller (1979) showing that West Indian girls were more active and persistent in seeking teachers' attention than boys.

These apparent contradictions may be explained partly by whether the research specifically studies, in 'normal' classroom life, pupil initiation of interactions, interaction in total, or interactions initiated by teachers. Also the age of the pupils may be important. For example, it seems possible that adolescent sexuality, which is sharply gender structured, may contribute to secondary school girls becoming less inclined to initiate interactions with their teachers in front of their male peers. However, Davies (1984) has shown that secondary school girls' actions are important in influencing the nature of school life. But it is in secondary schools where the power of peer pressure to conform to the often sexual, gender-structured, 'youth culture' reaches a peak (Connell et al, 1982:162-169). Hence, it is at secondary school where girls learn the subservient place many boys want them to occupy. However, given the egalitarian moves over the past fifteen years or so, it is also likely that some changes are occurring. Hence, more recent research, such as the present study, may be reflecting these changes.

In the teacher initiated interactions in Table 7.1, it is clear that the boys received more interactions from their teachers than did the girls. On average, 57 per cent of teacher initiated interactions went to boys. Brophy and Good (1974) discuss similar findings from early research in classrooms, so perhaps the children have changed more than the teachers. However, there are too many variations in the nature and circumstances of the various research studies over the years to conclude anything other than that further comparable research is required.

It is useful to turn to the interaction figures relating to some of the teachers referred to in previous chapters. Miriam Tate—who went from childhood on the farm, through marriage to a teacher, to becoming a teacher and school council member at Linfield—is a teacher with an egalitarian commitment. However, as we saw in the previous chapter, she is not able to rid herself of some of the deeply ingrained patterns of women's work. Table 7.2 shows that she treated her children almost equally in her initiated interactions. In this respect, Miriam Tate was the most equal teacher in the study. Table 7.2 also demonstrates how teacher initiated interaction scores can vary from day to day. Such variations are not entirely due to the teacher because pupils often behave in ways which encourage their teachers to initiate interactions with them. This is usually the case when matters of discipline or encouragement are called for.

Miriam Tate's girls initiated considerably more interactions with her than did the boys. Table 7.2 shows that 58 per cent of pupil initiated interactions came from these five and six year old girls. This pattern was consistent for each day except the fifth, when the

Table 7.2 Interaction scores for Miriam Tate's prep class at Linfield

Day	Teacher initiated interactions		Pupil initiated interactions	
	male recipient	female recipient	male	female
1	7.2 (47%)	8.9 (53%)	1.8 (38%)	3.0 (62%)
2	6.5 (57%)	4.9 (43%)	2.3 (40%)	3.5 (60%)
3	7.8 (52%)	7.3 (48%)	2.2 (39%)	3.4 (61%)
4	6.7 (60%)	4.4 (40%)	1.1 (42%)	1.5 (58%)
5	13.5 (49%)	14.1 (51%)	3.4 (49%)	3.6 (51%)
Weekly total	41.7 (51%)	39.6 (49%)	10.8 (42%)	15.0 (58%)
Daily mean	8.3 (51%)	7.9 (49%)	2.2 (42%)	3.0 (58%)

scores were almost equal. The conclusion from this class is that, although her own initiated interactions are almost equal, the girls had more interactions with her than did the boys. However, given the complexity of interpersonal relationships on a school classroom, it is difficult to tell to what extent Miriam Tate's background and egalitarian beliefs were responsible for these interaction patterns.

Carmel Walls and Donna Morton taught the composite prep, one and two grade at Tordale including children the same age as Miriam Tate's class, with children from the next two levels in addition. Donna Morton spent most of her teaching time with the class, but it was Carmel Walls who maintained the continuous influence over the children. Carmel Walls was relatively unconcerned with egalitarian issues in education, but Donna Morton was one of the most committed teachers to egalitarianism at either school.

Table 7.3 shows somewhat different patterns of teacher initiated interactions in Carmel Walls and Donna Morton's class from those of Miriam Tate's class, shown in Table 7.2. In the former the boys consistently received more interactions from their teachers, and on one day, the third, the boys received 70 per cent of the teacher initiated interactions. Later, the discussion of the qualitative evidence helps to explain these daily patterns, but for the present it can be seen that, in general, the experience of being a boy in Carmel Walls and Donna Morton's class is quantitatively quite different from that

Table 7.3 Interaction scores for Carmel Walls and Donna Morton's preparatory, grade one and two class at Tordale

Day	Teacher initiated interactions		Pupil initiated interactions	
	male recipient	female recipient	male	female
1	14.1 (56%)	11.9 (44%)	4.9 (50%)	5.0 (50%)
2	21.1 (59%)	14.6 (41%)	3.8 (48%)	4.2 (52%)
3	24.1 (70%)	10.6 (30%)	5.7 (42%)	7.8 (58%)
4	9.4 (54%)	7.9 (46%)	1.6 (48%)	1.9 (52%)
5	15.0 (52%)	13.8 (58%)	2.6 (40%)	3.9 (60%)
Weekly total	83.7 (59%)	58.8 (41%)	18.6 (45%)	22.8 (55%)
Daily mean	16.7 (59%)	11.8 (41%)	3.7 (45%)	4.6 (55%)

of being a girl. However, the girls do show that they are more willing to initiate interactions with their teachers than the boys. The percentage of interactions they initiate (55%) is slightly lower than is the case for Miriam Tate's girls (58%), but the superiority over the boys continues. Tables 7.2 and 7.3 demonstrate the effect that a low pupil-teacher ratio has on the numbers of interactions between teachers and their pupils. Both classes averaged 22 children during the observation periods, but the inclusion of Donna Morton with Carmel Walls for over half of each day reduced the teacher-pupil ratio to 1:11. Consequently, the numbers of both teacher initiated and pupil initiated interactions were greater than in Miriam Tate's class. The number of teacher initiated interactions was 65 per cent greater and the number of pupil initiated interactions was 38 per cent greater.

The teacher who, along with Donna Morton, was the most egalitarian in her views was Marilyn Carmody. As shown previously, she is an engaging person and an energetic teacher, but not entirely free from using gender based assumptions in her teaching. She organises leisure contact between the Linfield staff, such as sports matches and barbecues, and endeavours to ensure that men and women participate in both the activities and the catering. When she feels it necessary she questions gender based or sexist assumptions and comments at staff meetings.

Table 7.4 shows the interaction figures for Marilyn Carmody's class of grade one and twos. She had about 27 children in her class during our observation period and sustained the highest level of teacher initiated interaction of any of the single teacher classes we observed. However, we can see that she favoured boys with more of her initiated interactions (55 per cent). The children responded similarly to the previous two classes and, in fact, recorded precisely the same percentages of male and female initiated interaction scores, 45 per cent and 55 per cent respectively, as for Carmel Walls and Donna Morton's class at Tordale.

In reviewing the figures from these three classes, which are taught by the three teachers with the most avowedly egalitarian principles, two patterns emerge: the girls initiate more interactions with their teachers than do the boys; and the teachers initiate more interactions with the boys—only marginally so in Miriam Tate's case. Given the egalitarian principles which drive some part of these teachers' work, one might expect that they would have the most favourable interaction scores with girls. They might be expected to be keen to encourage the girls, to compensate for contrary effects elsewhere. Although, one might also argue that a true egalitarian would strive for equal teacher initiated interaction scores, such as Miriam Tate's. However, the girls who obtained the greatest interaction scores with their teacher were in Patrick Kerner's grade five class.

Table 7.4 Interaction scores for Marilyn Carmody's grade one and two class at Linfield

Day	Teacher initiated interactions		Pupil initiated interactions	
	male recipient	female recipient	male	female
1	12.3 (64%)	6.9 (36%)	2.6 (39%)	4.0 (61%)
2	8.2 (56%)	6.5 (44%)	4.1 (52%)	3.8 (48%)
3	13.4 (53%)	11.7 (47%)	4.1 (43%)	5.5 (57%)
4	7.7 (48%)	8.4 (52%)	1.9 (53%)	1.7 (47%)
5	9.1 (53%)	8.1 (47%)	1.8 (39%)	2.8 (61%)
Weekly total	50.7 (55%)	41.6 (45%)	14.5 (45%)	17.8 (55%)
Daily mean	10.1 (55%)	8.3 (45%)	2.9 (45%)	3.6 (55%)

Table 7.5 shows the figures for Patrick Kerner's class; he had an average of 30 children in the class during the observation period. Patrick Kerner is one of the teachers who quietly follows the trend towards equal opportunity between the sexes. His wife works in insurance and they have no children at present, but plan to in the next two years. When they become parents he expects to retain his job and has modest aspirations for gaining promotion.

Patrick Kerner's initiated interaction scores with girls are three per cent higher at 52 than those for Miriam Tate, but are still close to equal. On days two and three the boys received slightly more teacher initiated interactions than the girls, but these are outweighed by the more substantial differences in favour of girls on the remaining three days. The pupil initiated scores show a marked superiority for the girls with almost two-thirds of these interactions emanating from them. A similar proportion of pupil initiated scores was recorded for girls in Stephanie Bell's class of grade three and four children at Tordale. She averaged 25 children in her class during the observation period and, as Table 7.6 shows, she initiated more interactions with boys than girls.

Stephanie Bell's marriage had broken up four years ago. At the time her three children were teenagers and she has been the custodial parent and breadwinner ever since. She maintained some traditionally gender divided views about the appropriate behaviour for

Table 7.5 Interaction scores for Patrick Kerner's grade five class at Linfield

Day	Teacher initiated interactions		Pupil initiated interactions	
	male recipient	female recipient	male	female
1	3.1 (48%)	3.3 (52%)	1.6 (38%)	2.6 (62%)
2	3.1 (51%)	3.0 (49%)	3.3 (42%)	4.5 (58%)
3	5.4 (51%)	5.2 (49%)	1.8 (31%)	4.0 (69%)
4	4.4 (44%)	5.5 (56%)	3.5 (38%)	5.8 (62%)
5	4.1 (47%)	4.7 (53%)	1.4 (33%)	2.9 (67%)
Weekly total	20.1 (48%)	21.7 (52%)	11.6 (36%)	19.8 (64%)
Daily mean	4.0 (48%)	4.3 (52%)	2.3 (36%)	4.0 (64%)

Table 7.6 Interaction scores for Stephanie Bell's grade three and four class at Tordale

Day	Teacher initiated interactions		Pupil initiated interactions	
	male recipient	female recipient	male	female
1	11.1 (63%)	6.6 (37%)	6.1 (38%)	10.0 (62%)
2	8.5 (55%)	7.0 (45%)	5.5 (38%)	8.8 (62%)
3	6.9 (57%)	5.2 (43%)	3.9 (35%)	7.4 (65%)
4	2.7 (60%)	1.8 (40%)	1.6 (49%)	1.7 (51%)
5	10.5 (52%)	9.6 (48%)	5.3 (40%)	8.0 (60%)
Weekly total	39.7 (57%)	30.2 (43%)	22.4 (40%)	35.9 (60%)
Daily mean	7.9 (57%)	6.0 (43%)	4.5 (40%)	7.2 (60%)

boys and girls. However, she also incorporated some contemporary feminist terms in her discussions. For example, she identified one parent as a 'male chauvinist pig' because of his attitudes and actions toward both herself and his wife. She saw sharp, unacceptable discrepancies between the sexes on some occasions, but retained others—such as 'ladies first' courtesies—in her teaching.

Table 7.6 shows that Stephanie Bell initiated considerably more interactions with boys than girls. This is consistent with Carmel Walls and Donna Morton's class (Table 7.2) and together they comprise the first five of the seven grades at Tordale. On this basis, Tordale primary school boys consistently received more interactions than girls from their teachers. However, the Tordale girls initiated from 55 to 60 per cent of the pupil initiated interactions.

From the Linfield classes we have reviewed so far, we can see some similarities between the two schools. In each class it is the teachers who initiated more interactions than pupils. Up to almost three times as many interactions emanated from each teacher as from the 22 to 30 pupils. So the higher numbers of interactions that girls initiated can be offset by teachers who initiated more interactions with boys. In the case of Marilyn Carmody's class (Table 7.4) the percentages show a neat symmetry, with boys receiving 55 per cent of teacher initiated interactions and the girls initiating 55 per cent of the pupil initiated interactions. However, a summing of both types of interactions shows that the boys were involved in 65.2 interactions to the girls' 59.4, which gives the boys 52 per cent of all the interactions. But the boys did not always receive noticeably greater numbers of teacher initiated interactions, in one case (Table 7.2) things were close to equal and in another (Table 7.5) the girls were slightly ahead. In contrast, in the classes reviewed so far, the girls are consistently major initiators of interactions with their teachers. We shall look at some of the qualitative evidence to explain these patterns later in the chapter, but at this stage one could be forgiven for thinking that an affirmative action programme for Tordale and Linfield boys is in order! However, the remaining tables tell a different story.

Mary Thomson, who has a class of 26 grade three children at Linfield, is a mother of six who helps run the family farm. Table 7.7 shows that she consistently initiated more interactions with boys than girls and that the boys initiated more interactions with her. Although the previous classes we have reviewed show some relationship between the sex of pupil recipients and initiators—for example, Patrick Kerner (Table 7.5) had the highest initiation scores with girls and they initiated more interactions with him than girls in other classes—the relationship is not entirely consistent across the classes. However, Mary Thomson's class is the first to show boys as the main initiators of interactions in addition to being the main recipients. The girls initiate slightly fewer interactions with their teacher than do the boys, however, they only receive 40 per cent of the teacher initiated interactions.

Table 7.7 Interaction scores for Mary Thomson's grade three class at Linfield

Day	Teacher initiated interactions		Pupil initiated interactions	
	male recipient	female recipient	male	female
1	8.1 (59%)	5.7 (41%)	4.9 (52%)	4.5 (48%)
2	8.4 (59%)	5.9 (41%)	3.3 (55%)	2.7 (45%)
3	8.4 (64%)	4.7 (36%)	3.5 (54%)	3.0 (46%)
4	5.3 (58%)	3.9 (42%)	3.9 (58%)	2.8 (42%)
5	4.9 (61%)	3.1 (39%)	2.1 (48%)	2.3 (52%)
Weekly total	35.1 (60%)	23.3 (40%)	17.7 (53%)	15.3 (47%)
Daily mean	7.0 (60%)	4.7 (40%)	3.5 (53%)	3.1 (47%)

It is difficult to grade teachers according to their commitment to egalitarian views about gender, but one would suggest that Mary Thomson was one of the least committed, especially to many of the 'new wave' curricula and practices espoused within contemporary education. It is also difficult to assess the effect of such ideological commitment upon a teacher's practice. Stephanie Bell and Mary Thomson, both older teachers, are more traditional in their views about the lives of men and women, and they consistently initiated more interactions with boys than girls. However, both these women are 'battlers' who, in different ways, have performed domestic, parenting and breadwinning work beyond that which is usually expected of women. Other teachers, such as Donna Morton and Marilyn Carmody are much more vociferous about their ideological commitment and do shape their teaching activities in accordance. However, their interaction scores demonstrate that they are not able to sustain equality in their own initiated interactions.

Helen Hansen is a younger teacher who complained about the domination of Linfield's senior positions by men. She sees males as being behind many of her difficulties in life including her powerlessness in the school and her divorce. However, she expressed little egalitarian commitment in her teaching, which is reflected in her interaction scores in Table 7.8. She initiated the second highest

Table 7.8 Interaction scores for Helen Hansen's grade six class at Linfield

Day	Teacher initiated interactions		Pupil initiated interactions	
	male recipient	female recipient	male	female
1	5.3 (60%)	3.5 (40%)	1.0 (67%)	0.5 (33%)
2	5.7 (65%)	3.1 (35%)	0.9 (50%)	0.9 (50%)
3	2.6 (53%)	2.4 (47%)	2.2 (50%)	2.2 (50%)
4	5.5 (63%)	3.2 (37%)	1.9 (54%)	1.6 (46%)
5	8.7 (67%)	4.2 (33%)	2.2 (45%)	2.7 (55%)
Weekly total	27.8 (62%)	16.3 (38%)	8.2 (51%)	7.9 (49%)
Daily mean	5.6 (62%)	3.3 (38%)	1.6 (50%)	1.6 (50%)

percentage of interactions (62%) with boys of any teacher in the study and received slightly more pupil initiated interactions from boys than girls.

The two male teachers in the classroom observations adopted relatively similar positions with regard to equality of opportunity. Neither Patrick Kerner nor Steve Weston is an avowed egalitarian, although both expressed more egalitarian commitment than teachers such as Mary Thomson, Stephanie Bell and Helen Hansen. We have seen that Patrick Kerner's interaction scores (Table 7.5) favoured girls more than any other teacher. Conversely, Steve Weston's interaction scores in Table 7.9 represent the worst position for girls. He had a class of 29 grade three children and he initiated 64 per cent of his interactions with boys. Likewise he received 58 per cent of the pupil initiated interactions from boys.

Although Steve Weston and Patrick Kerner expressed relatively similar views about equal opportunity, their everyday lives and classroom practices have some quite different elements. In contrast to Patrick Kerner, Steve Weston is single and removed from the practical conditions of living with a woman engaged in a career. He is interested in music and dancing, especially country dancing with its attendant gender divisions, which he teaches to the children. Patrick Kerner is interested in and teaches sport, which also contains

Table 7.9 Interaction scores for Steve Weston's grade four class at Linfield

Day	Teacher initiated interactions		Pupil initiated interactions	
	male recipient	female recipient	male	female
1	5.8 (67%)	2.9 (33%)	2.0 (57%)	1.5 (43%)
2	7.3 (59%)	5.0 (41%)	4.1 (55%)	3.4 (45%)
3	5.5 (74%)	1.9 (26%)	4.3 (64%)	2.4 (36%)
4	2.2 (59%)	1.5 (41%)	2.9 (60%)	1.9 (40%)
5	9.4 (61%)	5.9 (39%)	2.2 (51%)	2.1 (49%)
Weekly total	30.2 (64%)	17.2 (36%)	15.5 (58%)	11.3 (42%)
Daily mean	6.0 (64%)	3.4 (36%)	3.1 (58%)	2.3 (42%)

many gender divisions, but he involves both sexes in his teaching. Such non-sexist teaching of sport is Ministry of Education and federal government policy and he willingly puts this into practice. These differences between Patrick Kerner and Steve Weston may help explain the differences in the interaction scores for their classes.

Across each of the individual class tables we have reviewed there are links between the lives and ideological positions of the teachers and their interaction scores in the classroom. Those who are most inclined to an egalitarian position discriminate less in favour of boys in their initiation of interactions. However, in these teachers' classes the girls usually dominate the pupil initiation of interactions. Those teachers who are least egalitarian discriminate more in favour of boys and the boys have a slight advantage in the pupil initiation of interactions. These links are not perfect and some classes have interaction patterns which vary from or over-emphasise this trend. For example, Patrick Kerner and Steve Weston do not represent the two extremes of egalitarian views, yet Tables 7.5 and 7.9 represent the two extremes of interaction scores. Similarly, Stephanie Bell is more traditionally sexist than her interaction scores would suggest (Table 7.6) and Donna Morton is one of the most egalitarian teachers in ideology and practice, although her scores suggest otherwise (Table 7.3). In Donna Morton's case the interaction scores only partially reflect her ideological position because Carmel Walls spent more time with the class than she did. However, in each case one needs to recognise that the children play an important part in affecting the interaction scores for each class.

In all the tables we can identify some patterns which are important to understanding the ways in which gender becomes a feature of classroom life. In every case we can see that, irrespective of the actual scores and percentages, girls always have higher percentages as initiators of interactions than as recipients; the opposite is the case for boys: they always have a higher score as recipients than as initiators. This pattern is clear in Table 7.1 where both schools have boys with higher scores as recipients of teacher initiated interactions and girls have higher scores for pupil initiated interactions. On the basis of these figures one might conclude that teachers discriminate in favour of boys by initiating twelve to sixteen percentage points more interactions with them than with the girls. One might also conclude that the girls are more assertive in class by virtue of their initiating six to twelve percentage points more interactions with their teachers than do the boys. The following section shows that such conclusions are simplistic and misleading.

Interactions: the story

Reducing selected classroom interactions to scores or percentages strips away the purpose and meaning of the interactions. In previous chapters many of the ordinary features of working and school life are shown to be vested with subtle, rich and powerful meanings, which are shaped by the gender structures of society and form part of an unfolding process of constructing future gender structures. We need to expose the nature of the interactions in the previous tables in order to understand and explain their relationship to the *gender agenda* of schooling. It emerges that the interaction scores and percentages provide only a part of the story, albeit a useful one.

In the corner

As I park my car in the Tordale school carpark I see Martin coming down the hill on his way to school. From one hand he trails a well worn school bag adorned with biro graffiti and in the other he has a thin stick with which he flails leaves and grass as he goes. Some hydrangea blooms hang enticingly over a fence and I anticipate Martin decapitating a few and showering the pathway with petals. He thinks better of it and goes for some grass instead.

The carnage Martin leaves strewn along his path is symptomatic of the way the teachers and pupils feel he behaves at school. He has a short 'pudding basin' haircut, ragged trousers, scuffed shoes and a grubby T-shirt. He is slightly overweight, but otherwise of normal stature for an eight year old, grade three boy. One of Martin's difficulties is that although he should be in Stephanie Bell's grade three and four class he is barely coping with grade two work in Carmel Walls's and Donna Morton's composite prep, one and two class. In their class he is bigger than the other children and has no friends: popularity is just not his strong suit.

Martin discards his stick outside the school gates and walks across the grass towards a group of boys playing cricket. I walk inside the school to prepare for another day of observing in Martin's class.

After the children arrive in the classroom, Carmel Walls gives out their writing folders. Martin kneels on his chair and sprawls himself across the table in a bid to talk to the other grade two children seated in the group. Carmel Walls positions herself behind him, shifts on to her left arm the pile of folders she is carrying and smacks him on the bottom with her free hand. She yells, 'Sit down properly, Martin'. He looks at her and grins as he slips back to sit on his chair. Within seconds he is out of his seat and sharpening his pencil at the fixed sharpener on a table near the front of the class. A queue forms behind Martin as he winds the pencil sharpener handle around and around, removes it, inspects it, then inserts it again for another cycle of sharpening and inspecting. A full size pencil is rapidly reduced to a stub. When he inspects the pencil tip for the third time, some childen in the queue become impatient and try to shove him aside. Martin uses his weight to fend them off with his hip. The noise from the queue attracts Donna Morton's attention: 'Martin, if you don't behave you'll be in the corner'. He whips his pencil out of the sharpener and sits down at his place.

The 'corner' is Martin's other place in the class. I found that he spent many hours there during the course of the week. The 'corner' is at the rear of the class and is formed out of cupboards and bookcases. Inside, the floor area is about a metre square and the entrance is a gap between the bookcases towards the rear. It had been tailor made for Martin by the teachers in an attempt to isolate him from his audience. The 'corner' is less than two metres from me and when Martin is in 'residence' I am the only person who can see him. Before Martin is sent to the 'corner' today, he is reprimanded for playing with his yo-yo, yelled at by Donna Morton for not working and disciplined for deliberately falling to the ground during some stretching exercises.

Once in the corner Martin is expected to continue his work whilst sitting on the floor. Sometimes he works for a while, but more often he occupies himself by adding graffiti to his belongings or his person, removing thin pieces of wood from the cupboard backs or exercising some of his personal habits. Occasionally a teacher checks on him and sometimes he comes out of the corner to show his work to a teacher or ask her a question.

The time comes for the children to change their readers. Carmel Walls sits at the front of the class as the children who wish to change their readers bring them to her. She checks to see that the book has been signed by one of the child's parents and usually asks the child to read some of it to her or describe the story. Another book is then exchanged for the child to read at home. Martin, on hearing that readers could be exchanged, slips out of the 'corner' and into a passing group of children as they were going to collect their readers. He returns to the class at speed and, by-passing the queue of children, goes straight to Carmel Walls. Martin pushes his book on to her lap. Carmel Walls is annoyed at his intrusion and after she quickly checks and finds that his book has not been signed she upbraids him: 'I don't change unsigned books and it's rude to interrupt'. Martin is sent back to the corner.

On his way back to the corner Martin stops at a table where some grade one children are working and looks at what they are doing. Emma calls out to Carmel Walls: 'Miss, Martin is being silly'. As the teacher looks up, Martin takes off for his 'corner'; Carmel Walls says nothing but she glares after him.

Soon it is lunchtime and Martin is allowed out of the corner to get his lunch and bring it to the class with the other children. The children sit on the floor to eat their lunches. Most children have plastic containers with sandwiches, and perhaps a cake, biscuits or fruit. Martin has a paper bag from which he removes the archetypal 'door-step' sandwich. He tears the sandwich apart, bites a large piece out of the centre and proceeds to chew it while maintaining continuous movement in his seat. He talks to other children and Carmel Walls says, 'Don't talk with your mouth full, Martin'. Martin eats the centre out of his sandwich and then lobs the crusts into the rubbish bin. He returns to sit on the mat next to Anna and asks her for the cake she is about to return to her container. She gives it to him and he quickly eats it. Carmel Walls sees Martin eating the cake and asks Anna, 'You gave him one of your cakes, Anna?' Anna replies, 'It was burnt on the top.' The teacher nods.

After their lunchtime play in the school grounds the children are back in the classroom. They sit chatting while waiting for the teachers to present the next piece of work. Rod Miles enters the class and the children become silent. The principal looks stern and asks the teachers if he can talk to the class. He addresses the class and explains that one of the grade five girls in his class has complained that Martin punched her at lunchtime. The principal readily collects incriminating evidence from the children about Martin who initially pleads innocence. He swiftly changes his defence to one of retaliation, on the grounds that he had been hit first by the girl, but it is to no avail. Rod Miles pronounces him guilty and issues him with a warning: 'Now listen, Martin. I shall tell my girls that they can hit you once if you hit them. One hit will probably be enough from some of my bigger girls. We shall have to pick you up with a vacuum cleaner afterwards'.

After Rod Miles departs, Carmel Walls continues talking to the children about the virtues of being 'nice to one another'. Martin remains relatively quiet for the rest of the afternoon and although he is cajoled several times he escapes being sentenced to another spell in the 'corner'.

Teachers' trouble

Martin presents an extreme example of the trouble that is caused by some boys, and fewer girls, during the course of a school day.

Martin was seen by the Tordale staff as the most difficult boy in the school and, from all appearances, the pupils, and probably Martin, agreed. It is difficult to discern what made Martin especially cussed. The staff pointed to his parents as the culprits—as teachers usually do—however, his behaviour was severe enough to warrant a school psychologist to see him regularly. For half a day Martin's classroom interactions were recorded separately. During this period he received a quarter of the interactions initiated by the teachers and nearly all these interactions were concerned with discipline or control. This means that if Martin were not in the class then the volume of teacher initiated interactions going to boys would be reduced, probably to the extent that the present 62 per cent in Table 7.3 would approach 50 per cent.

This raises the problem of the extent to which teachers can be said to initiate interactions when it is clear that they are often responding to an event in the classroom. Jackson (1968) has demonstrated that classroom life is often frantic for teachers; they spend much of their time reacting to events rather than dictating them. Classroom life at Linfield and Tordale could be seen in this way; often the teachers were diligently scanning the classroom to see who was doing what and then reacting to encourage, assist, praise or remonstrate where they felt it necessary. However, in their work as teachers they are expected to initiate events and enact the curriculum. Also, as teachers, they are able to make selections and choices concerning their actions which shape classroom events. In the previous chapter it was shown that gender played an important part in shaping those selections and choices and, thereby, constructing future gender relationships in the rising generation.

Gender also shapes the actions of children to the extent that teachers anticipate different behaviour from boys and girls. Donna Morton commented that the 'boys are boys and the girls are girls' in the ways they behaved at Tordale. As she is opposed to sexism and advocates equal opportunity, she dislikes this aspect of the children at the school. Nevertheless she has to contend with what she perceives as a traditional gender division in the attitudes and behaviour of the children. Donna Morton chooses to try and modify the children's attitudes and behaviour in line with her egalitarian beliefs, but children such as Martin make this task immensely difficult.

In some people's minds, Martin represents an extreme form of what is accepted, or at least expected, of boys. Ramsay (1983) argues that boys who are boisterous and aggressive conform to teachers' expectations and that girls who are quiet and docile do likewise. Davies (1984:172) refers to other writers who make similar claims, not only about teachers, but also about the boys and girls' acceptance of such divisions. In particular, she criticises Willis's (1977) 'conservative sexism' in his attribution of all that is 'interesting, amusing and active' to males. At Linfield and Tordale many of the teachers referred to the traditional divisions between the actions of boys and girls. Often it was teachers, such as Donna Morton, who have some egalitarian commitment who made such points. The more conservative teachers were less likely to talk about differences in boys and girls' behaviour, but it seemed clear that they both expected and accepted any such differences without question. For the conservative teachers the idea of critically challenging traditional gender divisions in their lives or in the lives of others never entered their consciousness: it was not an issue. It was, however, becoming increasingly difficult for them to adopt this position in the face of the plethora of information they were receiving from people and organisations, that challenged traditional gender divisions. Indeed, the presence of our research project in their school is likely to have contributed to this process.

Although Martin represented an extreme case, it was generally true that the teachers allocated more of their initiated interactions to the disciplining of boys than of girls. It was common for teachers to address disciplinary comments to groups of boys in the form of, 'right you boys, be quiet' or 'you boys won't go out to play until you've cleared up that mess'. Similar comments were addressed to groups of girls, but they were far less frequent than for boys. It was clear that if disciplinary comments were removed from the teacher initiated interaction scores then the distributions to boys and girls would be closer to equal.

In contemporary literature on the subject, it is usual for the classroom interaction discrepancy in favour of boys to be seen as an indication of girls' disadvantage at school (Commonwealth Schools Commission, 1984:33). However, to the extent that this additional teacher attention is made up of negative, disciplinary language, one may question whether this is entirely the case. Partly, the answer lies in the different expectations teachers have of boys' and girls' behaviour (Evans, 1982a). As some aspects of the trouble boys cause their teachers are seen as typical of being 'just a boy', the admonishments they receive are not necessarily construed as being damaging to their self-esteem as boys. It must also be said that some trouble is expected from girls and children in general, perhaps one could best describe this as being the sorts of trouble which 'kids' cause adults. However, a child such as Martin, is not being 'a kid' or 'just a boy'; Martin is severely testing and challenging his teachers and other children at the school. Martin encourages a high number of teacher initiated interaction scores to boys in his class, but the consequent disadvantage is probably shared by every boy and girl in the class. Girls who are as difficult as Martin—a girl in Helen Hansen's grade six at Linfield, who in later years was excluded from her secondary school on the insistence of the staff, made Martin appear almost reasonable in comparison—have a similar effect on their schools. Due to the gender relationships inherent in school discipline, where it is often male teachers who are seen as the prevailing authority figures, troublesome girls are even more difficult to cope with. This is another argument for a fair representation of women in the senior positions in schools.

Teachers' favourites

The resurgence of feminism has affected the nature and interpretation of classroom research. Some contemporary research, mostly by women, focuses on the differences in classroom experiences between boys and girls (for example, Stanworth, 1981) and argues that girls are consistently disadvantaged. However, earlier research, often by men, argued a different case. In their monumental review of classroom research up to the early seventies, Brophy and Good found that teachers in the USA overestimated the achievement ability of girls and underestimated that of boys. It was said that, 'boys are... more active in seeking and getting contacts with teachers...but also are criticized more for misbehaviour (1974:231). They cited Palardy (1969) as finding, '...that boys can learn as well as girls if properly taught' and they concluded, 'Perhaps in the future...school success will be expected of young boys as well as young girls'. The contrast between these earlier studies and the contemporary ones is clear, although the findings are not so dissimilar. The explanation lay in the more critical perceptions that feminism has fostered and its concern to substantiate girls' disadvantage. There are, however, inequalities brought to both girls (mostly) and to boys by the gender structures and processes which exist in school and society.

Reports in Australia, such as *Girls, School and Society* (Commonwealth Schools Commission, 1975), show that on broad measures of educational attainment, such as examination pass rates, retention rates etc., girls are equal to or better than boys. However, the effect of gender on the choices girls make at school, the sexist ways in which curriculum materials have been produced and the profound effects of society, media and family values, leave girls to succeed in areas which often do not connect with viable breadwinning careers. The reports *Girls and Tomorrow* (Commonwealth Schools Commission, 1984) and *Technological Change in Australia* (1980) show that fewer girls choose mathematics and sciences than boys. Although there are other important subjects, mathematics and sciences provide the basis for further education and employment in many existing and emerging careers. Boys are encouraged from an early age to play with toys and games which develop their physical, manual and mechanical skills (Delamont, 1980a). In fact, toy shops and toy manufacturers represent some of the least challenged agents of sexism in society. Girls are largely left out of developing such skills and during their secondary schooling, when adolescent peer pressure is at its height, they often leave mathematics and sciences, except biology, to the boys. In effect, the *gender agenda* of schooling provides for mathematics and sciences to be the boys' topics and home economics/domestic science and commerce to be the girls' topics (Taylor, 1980, 1982).

Another element of classroom processes which impinges on the *gender agenda* of schooling is teachers' preferences for teaching boys rather than girls. Davies (1984:70) found that when forced to make a choice, 71 per cent of teachers in her study preferred to teach boys. Davies acknowledges the inconsistencies between this response and the fact that boys generally cause more trouble for teachers than girls. Similar inconsistencies have been reported elsewhere (Clarricoates, 1978; Spender, 1980). In the present study we found that most teachers said they had no preference, but with the remaining few teachers there was a slight preference for boys.

The teachers were also asked to nominate the children who were best at mathematics, English and sport. Overall the teachers at Tordale and Linfield nominated slightly more boys than girls, but it was also found that both the degree of egalitarian ideology which the teachers expressed and the age of the pupils concerned correlated with the equalness of their nominations. For example, Helen Hansen who was one of the more conservative younger teachers, said that the best pupils at mathematics in her grade six class were boys and she observed that 'the girls are just not as quick at problem solving'. Susan O'Reilly nominated boys and girls equally and said there was 'no real difference between them in grade one, it's when they get older that they start all that macho business'. At Tordale the boys were nominated as best at mathematics and the girls at English and sport. In fact, the girls' disinterest and lack of competence in mathematics had been a matter of discussion between staff and some parents immediately prior to the research commencing at the school.

The perception of girls as being good at sport was also a feature of the nominations at Linfield. At both schools some individual girls, such as Jenny whose race opened this book, were said to be outstanding at athletics, swimming or as 'all-rounders'. Some teachers were moved to suggest that they believed these girls were future national representatives. At neither school was a boy spoken of in these terms. Given that we are discussing some individual girls in two primary schools the explanation could be that this is pure coincidence. Boys were nominated as being good at particular sports, soccer was often mentioned and sometimes Australian football and basketball; girls were never nominated in these sports. The division between the types of sports for which girls and boys are nominated is not a coincidence. The team games the boys played are predominantly men's games in the adult world. The girls who were nominated could succeed and develop in their sports individually, without having to depend on a team of 'mates' for their participation.

Seeking affirmation

Perhaps the most unusual finding from the classroom observations in relation to previous research in the field, is that the girls initiated more interactions with their teachers than did the boys (see Table 7.1). Most research has found, as Brophy and Good (1974) concluded, that boys are more active in seeking their teachers' attention. As was mentioned at the beginning of this chapter, Davies has cited Fuller's more recent research in Britain as finding that: 'Typically, the girls would call loudly from their seats...If this did not work, it was not uncommon to leave their desk, take their query to the teacher and follow him or her about if necessary' (1984:194).

We found that girls were more likely than boys to seek the teacher's attention in order to have their work checked, to affirm that they were proceeding correctly or to seek permission to do something. There was a greater instance of girls raising their hands to ask, 'Miss Walls, is this all right?' or 'Mr Kerner, is this how you do it?' or 'Miss Carmody can I change my book?'. This type of attention seeking, which conforms neatly to approved school behaviour, contrasts markedly with Martin's methods of obtaining attention. The nature of the difference in the teacher initiated interaction scores for boys and girls does not suggest that the girls are being any more assertive than the boys. Rather it suggests that they were more in need of affirmation, perhaps because they were less confident or because they were more concerned to get their school work right.

* * *

Throughout the individual class interaction tables in this chapter there are differences in the male and female initiated and recipient interactions. The egalitarian commitment of the teachers correlates with the way the interaction scores are distributed between the sexes. So the classes where the girls had the highest teacher initiated and pupil initiated interaction scores were generally those where the teachers expressed the greatest egalitarian commitment. Therefore, it was the case that girls were able to seek and obtain more affirmation from 'egalitarian' than other teachers. The important message here is that the teachers' egalitarian commitment affects their teaching and general behaviour in class in ways which change the girls' initiation of interactions with them.

This raises the question of what happens to the boys in classes where the girls dominate the interactions? Are they being squeezed out of some of their primary schooling by the girls in, perhaps, a similar way to the girls in the classes where the boys dominate? Or does the nature of gender relationships in schooling mean that, in the former types of class, the girls are receiving a form of compensation for other, especially subsequent, inequities? These questions fall outside the scope of the present research, however, our observations at the schools did not show that the girls dominated the boys in other respects. Although there were instances where particular girls or groups of girls were able to shape the *agenda* of their school lives more powerfully than others, it was more common for boys to shape the *agenda* for activities outside of the classroom at lunch and recess times. Many of the games played were 'male' sports which groups of boys kept largely, but not always exclusively, to themselves. For example, at Tordale, there were several lunchtimes when cricket was played by a mixed sex group of children, but the girls were always substantially outnumbered.

As with all gender and other social relationships, whether in the family, workplace, community or school classroom, it is important to endeavour to understand not only the 'objective' measures of those relationships, such as interaction scores, numbers of participants etc., but also the nature, history and meanings embedded in those 'objective' measures. Without such an understanding not only are inadequate, or even incorrect, conclusions likely to be drawn, but also the framing of social and educational policy may be misguided and incorrectly evaluated. To exemplify the difficulties involved in these processes, perhaps the reader could decide which class in the previous tables they think is best from the viewpoint of equal opportunity. Is it Patrick Kerner's where girls did so well? Or is it Miriam Tate's where her initiated interactions are the most equal? Or is it Helen Hansen's where the pupil initiated interactions are the most equal? Or should we turn back to Chapter 4 to find out more about the particular teachers before we decide? Whatever we decide, the children of Linfield and Tordale have no choice in the matter.

8 Conclusion: new *agendas* for old

This book focuses on the people whose lives are directly related to primary schools and shows how they each represent an embodiment of the experiences and circumstances which have shaped or are shaping their lives. Gender is crucial to understanding both these experiences and circumstances and the processes through which people construct their own meanings and actions in these respects. The parts that parents, teachers and pupils play in the enactment of primary school life are examined throughout this book. However, the strength and pervasiveness of gender differentiation in society rests in the interconnectedness of the parts played not only by teachers, parents and pupils, but also more broadly through the mass media, religion, sports, employers, government agencies, etc. It also rests on the interconnectedness between domestic, parenting and breadwinning work. The essential nature of domestic and parenting work is obscured by the reverence shown to breadwinning. The traditional allocation of these forms of work to women and men, respectively, is a cultural process formed partly through the *gender agendas* of schooling.

In this concluding chapter three themes are presented which help to make the interconnections between the parts played by the people involved with primary schools and elements of the social world outside of the school. The first section deals with *gender agendas* and how they unfold and are reconstructed from one generation to the next, partly through primary schooling. The second section reviews the *gender agendas* to be found at Linfield and Tordale schools. And the final section looks to the problems and possibilities for providing an *agenda* more free of gender differentiation

Gender agendas as social reconstruction

At Linfield and Tordale *gender agendas* impinge on social life through several different forms. Within the school, each member has a personal *gender agenda*, a collective school *gender agenda* and a broader societal *agenda*. Personal *gender agendas* are constructed out of previous experience and circumstances. They are constructed from the viewpoint of each person's sex. The physiological characteristics of sex at birth mark the commencement of a segregated life in a way that differences in class, religion or ethnicity do not match. One's personal *gender agenda* is usually inherited in a primitive but unswerving form at birth. The names, name-tags, blankets, greeting cards, etc. are the first artefacts from a culture historically comprised of powerful *gender agendas*. The personal *gender agendas* of individual teachers, parents and pupils reflect their unique combinations and interpretations of their experiences and circumstances, but largely conform to the *gender agendas* of society.

Within the schools there are collective *gender agendas* which reflect both the members' *agendas* and those of society at large. Such collective *gender agendas* do not reflect a symmetrical consensus among the members or with the society. Tordale and Linfield provide many examples where individuals and groups have disliked, resisted or endeavoured to modify collective *gender agendas*. In fact, an element of any *gender agenda* is the contestation, in addition to differentiation, which takes place between male and female. This was seen in operation at council, staff, and election meetings.

Societal *gender agendas* shroud school and personal life mainly through bureaucratic and legal arms of government; media, arts, play, sport and leisure; and religion, politics and economics. It is difficult to imagine any element of social life which is devoid of gender. However, the extent to which people, both individually and collectively, accept or conform to societal *gender agendas* depends on the degrees of coercion and enforcement applied, and on the individual's capacity to resist them. The gender differentiation in societal *agendas* is often massive. The divisions embedded within domestic and parenting labour, which the people of Tordale and Linfield live out daily, largely exclude men from responsibility and access to this work and force women to shoulder the burdens. To a lesser extent breadwinning labour is similarly gender-differentiated, especially where careers and seniority are concerned. Here men are expected to shoulder the burdens and women are accorded only marginal or restricted occupations.

Agendas represent constructs of knowledge, attitudes and values which are fragments of culture. Especially in their personal and community forms, *agendas* are readily influenced by the people who surround them. Children's *agendas* are affected by the experiences provided by adults, for example, their knowledge about the participation of men and women in different forms of labour was cited by them in their accounts of what they recognised as relevant for themselves. *Agendas* also contain prescriptions for appropriate action and behaviour. Hence, *gender agendas* require that men and women, boys and girls, respond in different ways according to their sex. Such gender differentiation includes power relationships which usually accord men power over women. Some mothers at Tordale expressed their subservience to men such as the principal and council president. Some women teachers at Linfield said likewise about their relationships with men at the school.

In many respects the conception of *agenda* I am formulating here is a bridge between what Bourdieu refers to as the 'habitus' (1977), and the physical habitats in which people live. In the habitat there are objective artefacts, monuments, toys, documents etc., which chart a path for masculinity and femininity and reflect the gender differentiated physical worlds of men and women. In the subjective 'habitus' rest the internalised competencies, ways of knowing, perceptions, appreciations and actions which are very much the terrain of gender. *Gender agendas* represent a routinisation that stems from what Giddens (1984) calls the 'recursive nature of social life'. He suggests that this recursiveness is central to social structure and to its recreation. In terms of gender, recursiveness is endemic in Tordale and Linfield, and its recreation—or construction and reconstruction—is enduring. *Gender agendas* are constructed with and reconstructed on the 'objective' symbols of biological and physiological sex differences from which the 'subjective' cultural forms of masculinity and femininity take shape.

The construction and reconstruction of *gender agendas* are social processes which produce gender, in Berger and Luckmann's (1967) terms, as a 'socially constructed objective reality'. The various forms and levels of *gender agenda* are intertwined, layer upon layer, and bonded with the 'adhesives' of religion and morality. Such bonds are difficult to crack, let alone break. Their strength derives from their ubiquity. It is difficult to imagine a social setting in which gender does not act to shape the social processes and the thoughts and actions of the people involved. The prevailing circumstances are ones of patriarchy or male domination, although there are a few settings where there is a female dominated gender order (Matthews, 1984:13–15).

Gender as a form of structural inequality—constructed and reconstructed by people—involves both rules and resources (see Giddens, 1984:xxi). Essentially, rules about actions and behaviour, and resources in material and cultural forms—for example, knowledge and skills—are related or directed to men and women by virtue of their sex. In Tordale and Linfield, individuals' *gender agendas* do not bear a perfect symmetrical relationship to each other. Contradictions exist that lead to areas of contestation between members and groups in those communities. Some of the teachers' personal *gender agendas* are fired by concerns with feminism or social justice which contribute to friction between them and others whose *gender agendas* are constructed differently. The Blockies and Farmers at Tordale show how varying class and work interests can contribute to shaping *gender agendas* for individuals and communities. On occasions such interests coalesced neatly within the social *gender agenda*, but on others the class and work interests of Blockie and Farmer women vaporised their fluid links in sisterhood.

Government policy provides its own contradictory pressures. Equal opportunity, social justice and 'participation and equity' policies and programmes conflict with policies and programmes that increase the power of communities to construct and reconstruct their inequalities through schooling. It has to be recognised that, in effect, school communities are being empowered to reflect and press their own class, gender and ethnicity interests.

* * *

Due to the contradictions and contestation within and between *gender agendas*, the bonds between some *gender agendas* and others have begun to crack, especially though feminist contributions to areas such as equal opportunity legislation and procedures. Some *gender agendas* exist that challenge traditional notions of gender and provide people with ideas and practices about gender and gender order which are substantially egalitarian. Because such egalitarian *gender agendas* must exist alongside and within other more traditional *gender agendas* there is the potential for conflict and coercion. In particular, radical feminism constructs *gender agendas* which directly counter traditional, patriarchal forms of male domination. However, in so doing, it endeavours to construct female dominated gender orders. While this may be useful in shaking patriarchy to its foundations, it may leave other gender orders to be removed in the pursuit of equality between the sexes.

The old *gender agendas*

At Tordale and Linfield, old and existing *gender agendas* are imposed on the emerging ones. The primary schools play a part in, and provide a location for, the construction of emerging *gender agendas*. However, so do the families and communities of Tordale and Linfield which, in turn, are interconnected with the gender relationships and differentiation of the society at large. The teachers and parents conform to patterns of work set out in accordance with the old *gender agendas*—their parenting, domestic and breadwinning work exhibits features from the traditional pattern: mothers work at parenting their children and fathers only provide occasional, part-time parenting; mothers are morally responsible for their children, fathers are only residually responsible; mothers constitute community parenting groups, facilities and networks, fathers are strangers to these; women are expected to wash laundry, clean, cook, purchase food and household items, etc., men are not; women, especially mothers, are not required to be breadwinners, men are expected to be so; women are subservient in the workplace, men dominate; women's pay is secondary, men's is primary. The Tordale and Linfield communities are thriving examples of the traditional *gender agendas* in action and construction. The teachers are no exceptions; they conform as neatly as do the parents. Certainly, the nature of teaching as breadwinning does mean that the women teachers are better paid, educated, and employed than the women in the communities. But, in most *gender agendas*, teaching, especially primary teaching, is women's work and also it is the men teachers who dominate the organisational structures of both schools.

Tordale and Linfield schools work to reconstruct the old *gender agendas* into contemporary forms. The contemporary forms are rarely much different from the past, but they do incorporate recent symbols and meanings from contemporary culture. To the extent that there are recent symbols and meanings related to gender equality—for example, 'new wave' curriculum materials and sexually inclusive curricula—then these are interpreted and incorporated to varying degrees into the reconstruction of *gender agendas*. So, at Tordale and Linfield, there are examples of shifts in the interpretation and propagation of gender differences to some classes because their teachers have adopted fragments of the feminist critique of traditional gender practices. These teachers work alongside others who ignore or resist such critiques and who are largely reconstructing traditional *gender agendas*.

However, irrespective of the classroom practices of the teachers, their broader, everyday lives demonstrate considerable conformity to traditional *gender agendas*. They live out traditional *gender agendas* in their personal and public lives. They also anticipate and/or follow career and family paths which, broadly, conform to such *agendas*.

Although all teachers construct their own career and family circumstances, this is done in the context of the interlocking *gender agendas* which pervade their biographies and extend through their present lives and into the future they anticipate for themselves. The few teachers who attempt to be sexually inclusive in their teaching and interactions do so against the backdrop of their own gender segregated lives.

The hierarchical organisations of the schools—enshrined in policy documents and ministry edicts—are practical examples of male dominated gender orders. The authority, power and knowledge which is vested in the highest positions of the hierarchies reflects masculine notions of control, domination and politics. A *gender agenda* which is reconstructed to increase the participation of women in the operation of schools does not necessarily mean that such women will be able to share equally in the power, authority and knowledge. Women are numerically dominant in primary schools—they constitute the majority of staff, including ancillary staff, and they control the mothers' clubs and are the majority in parents' clubs. Mothers spend far more time in schools than do fathers, however, usually schools are controlled by a few fathers and male principals and teachers.

By using parents in these ways, the schools turn the parents into school-legitimated, living examples of traditional, gender segregated practices. This contributes to the reconstruction of traditional forms of *gender agenda* by the children.

The organisation of parents' work around schools is firmly gender segregated. However, the Tordale and Linfield schools and communities are not locations of uncontested gender relationships. A few mothers and teachers, mostly women, at the schools have personal *gender agendas* which, in some ways, run counter to the traditional forms. Significantly, it is almost exclusively middle class women (and a few such men) who offer these moderate challenges to traditional *gender agendas*.

Towards new *gender agendas*

This book shows how the everyday lives of children and adults on school communities are shaped by a series of interlocking *gender agendas*. The challenges to traditional gender segregation and sexism in schools come from several sources, especially from feminists, governments and unions. However, much of the emphasis is placed on what overtly occurs in the classroom. Tordale and Linfield show that the effects of these challenges are in evidence, but that they are minimal. Several reasons for such a minimal effect may be proffered. In Tordale and Linfield, the organisation of everyday life in the schools, families, communities and wider society provides an 'unofficial', but strongly legitimated, curriculum and pedagogy of gender. Because, in the immediate sense at least, the source of such pedagogies resides in the nature of school, community and family organisation, then the source of new *gender agendas* must also reside there. Oakley argues in her autobiography that, 'Politics, especially sexual politics, begin at home' (1984:199) and it is here that the teachers, parents and children inherit and transmit, learn and live their *gender agendas*.

If new *agendas* are to be constructed, wherein the constraints of gender are at least minimised to the extent that men and women are free to organise their lives irrespective of their sex, a revolution is required in the ways we organise work. Although there are other features of social life which also warrant challenge—the nature of marriage and family organisation, sport and religion are examples—by concentrating on work, the main engine of gender inequality will be addressed. For societies and their economies to be maintained each of the forms of work—domestic, parenting and breadwinning—are essential. However, breadwinning work is usually seen as the 'real', 'productive' work; domestic and parenting work—'housework' is the common, if slightly misleading, word—is rarely accorded its true value (Oakley, 1974a, 1974b). Domestic and parenting work are not accorded their true values largely because, through the alliance of patriarchy and capitalism, they are allocated to women and breadwinning to men. Of course, similar alliances exist outside of capitalism and also not all breadwinning work is allocated to men.

If the *gender agendas* of work are to be weakened or destroyed, there will need to be a removal of the moral imperative on women to be solely responsible for domestic and parenting work, and on men to be largely responsible for breadwinning. Men and women need to be responsible for, and have a right to perform, their own domestic, parenting and breadwinning labour. Hence, all forms of such labour must be shared by the adults who are responsible for them. This means that, from time to time, men and women, in their personal, social or working relationships, might choose freely to apportion their work in ways which suit their mutual interests. However, it does mean that adult breadwinning work should be organised in ways which recognises the rights and responsibilities of men and women to paid work and to care for children if they are parents. The breadwinning, usually male, 'workaholic' needs to be recognised as greedy and distorted in his acquisition of breadwinning work at the expanse of responsibilities to his domestic, and often parenting, work. 'Workaholism' is not a virtue, but working carefully at breadwinning, domestic labour and parenting should be.

This means reorganising employment so that all forms of work are shared fairly between the sexes; it also means redistributing wages and work hours. Present wage structures are based on traditional *gender agendas* of work. Wajcman and Rosewarne (1986) demonstrate that there have been some attempts at reconstructing wage structures by arguments based on the comparable worth of 'feminine' and 'masculine' forms of work. However, these are hampered by controls over wages by governments and the interests of some unions. An equitable organisation of work for men and women would go beyond restructuring wage differentials. It would recognise that men and women have a responsibility to parent their children. Hence, matters such as caring for a sick child, good childcare provision, and parental leave, need to be considered seriously by employers, governments, communities and, especially, the men who dominate these agencies and groups. Oakley argues, 'There is, after all, no reason why men should renounce the comforts of patriarchy other than that the women to whom they are attached require them to do so' (1984: 75). I would argue that there are good reasons for men to do this, aside from any moral commitment to equality, and these are concerned with their increased self worth as fathers, the benefits of shared childcare (see Russell, 1983), and a reduction in occupational stress through shared breadwinning responsibilities. However, part of Oakley's argument concerns the 'comforts' of men opting out of domestic labour. Here men need to be made 'uncomfortable' by the women in their lives and by any egalitarian men with whom they come into contact. Arguably, this 'discomfort' should be propagated through media and other campaigns which address the social justice concerns of the organisation of family life. In these ways an engine of gender inequality would be spiked.

At Tordale and Linfield the careers of teachers follow traditional, gender differentiated patterns. To remove the *gender agendas* involved in teaching careers requires the sorts of changes to work mentioned previously. However, if a new, more egalitarian, *gender agenda* is to be constructed for teaching careers, then not only do broad changes need to be made to the organisations of careers in educational bureaucracies, but also all teachers need to adopt a gender critical view of themselves, their actions and their social worlds. For example, male teachers should consider the way they exercise their parenting responsibilities when they become parents. They should make as much use of their 'family' leave entitlements as women teachers do when they become parents. Quite apart from the benefits to their own families and the equity issues involved, such an experience may improve their teaching, provide more work for unemployed teachers and give their pupils living examples of fathers doing their fair share of parenting work.

The ways teachers live out their careers provides a form of living curriculum for the school. The pupils observe the *gender agendas* of teachers' practices and use them in the construction of their own social realities. The hierarchical administrative, power and authority structures of Tordale and, especially, Linfield form part of the schools' *gender agendas*. The teachers' gender structured views about children also have an impact on the curricula and pedagogies they impose.

The manner in which teachers' careers are structured and practised forms another part of this *agenda*. Male teachers on school councils, in staff meetings and in relations with their female colleagues, need to reflect critically on the sources and consequences of the political and machismo games they play in living and furthering their careers. Female teachers in these circumstances need to be similarly critical, but with a view to challenging men and asserting themselves in their careers. The women teachers at Tordale and Linfield were gently defining themselves out of pursuing careers in teaching beyond the Band Two level. There were no women teachers at either school above this level who could be an example to female colleagues. In fact, the junior male teachers expressed similar reservations about becoming principals. Here lies one of the contradictions in the changes in education in recent years. The responsibilities of school principals have become more onerous—especially in terms of politicking between educational bureaucracies, school staff, parents and school councils—to the extent that the position of principal, particularly in larger schools like Linfield, is becoming so intensely demanding that many teachers are saying they will not apply for such promotions. The position of principal is changing to involve even more masculine activities than before. It is arguable that the men attracted to such positions will be those with no commitment to any form of new *gender agendas* in their lives. Their careers will be erected on traditional gender relationships: with women to wash their socks, feed them and their children, do their typing, take their minutes etc.

* * *

The State government's changes to school council powers include the option for a council to select its principal when a vacancy occurs. Taken together with the aforementioned 'masculine' changes to the work of principals, especially in relation to their responsibilities and dealings with their councils, and considering the way the Tordale and Linfield school councils work, it seems that the prospects are bleak for improving the number of women principals. The increases in the powers of school councils largely means giving greater power to the men in strongly gender divided communities. In effect, the prospect of equality between the sexes becomes more remote. If equity and social justice, including the removal of sexism and gender divisions, are to be pursued partly through education, then an understanding of the social processes involved is essential. Concentrating on educational matters, such as the curriculum or classroom interactions, to the exclusion of addressing the *gender agendas* embedded in the careers of teachers, the organisational politics of schools and communities, the mass media, the organisation of family and community life is sheer folly. Any gains made in the classroom, and Tordale and Linfield show that there are some gains, are washed away by the next incoming tide of gender segregated social life.

Some radical changes need to be considered to restructure teachers' careers if children are not to be confronted with traditional gender role models in the classroom. Previously it was argued that male teachers who become parents need to be encouraged to care for their young children. Corbett (1987) notes that in Denmark either parent is entitled to ten weeks leave on 90 per cent full pay after the initial maternity leave period of 18 weeks full pay. Furthermore she adds that in Poland fathers are entitled to three years paid leave until their child is four years of age. With sufficient changes to the ways we think of parenting, breadwinning and domestic work our own pay and leave conditions could be more usefully restructured. For teachers, perhaps, the present family leave provisions should include a payment to men at the end of each year of family leave. Women teachers should be given special support and encouragement to achieve senior positions. Maybe the senior positions in schools should be allocated so that both women and men are always represented. The nature of seniority and the occupational hazards of the traditional hierarchical model of seniority need critical review. There are also other aspects of the *gender agenda* of teachers' careers which warrant reviewing. The crucial point is that teachers' careers do not require reviewing solely to reconstruct the *gender agenda* of teaching; it is because of the influence these *gender agendas* have in constructing traditional *gender agendas* in the young that such a gender critical review is important.

A similar gender critical review of the relationship between schools, parents and adults is necessary if traditional *gender agendas* are to be challenged. The practices of schools which rely on and legitimate the traditional gender segregated forms of adult work should be seen as problematic. Governments and policy makers need to recognise that their cost-cutting and community involvement policies are used as incentives for schools and their communities to derive savings out of the 'voluntary exploitation' of women in canteens, sewing groups, etc. Perhaps thought should be given to paying unemployed young men and women to work part-time for schools to assist in these activities and in other support work.

The *gender agenda* of parents' lives is further reinforced by the increased demand for work—in effect, middle class, 'masculine' work—on school councils and sub-committees. The nature of this 'rational-bureaucratic' work makes it middle class; its organisation, scheduling and intersection with male dominated school hierarchies, make it 'masculine'. Large numbers of working-class women at Linfield never considered being a council member and some of the middle-class women at Tordale felt 'put down' by men when they did. The *gender agenda* of parenting and domestic work mitigates against mothers attending after school or evening meetings, especially ones which are long and have no deadline. In order to ensure equity in the participation of mothers and fathers in the work of schools each of these previous matters needs to be considered and changed. School councils are required to have minimum proportions of parent, teacher and, for secondary schools, student members. Perhaps each of these membership groups should have minimum proportions of men and women. The distribution of the sexes throughout the office bearers should also be considered. However, the broader issues concerning the nature and organisation of school council work and parental involvement in schools required gender critical review before membership changes can be effectively practised.

More fundamentally, the notion of participation in schools through the mechanism of extending the powers and responsibilities of school councils should be questioned. Linfield provides a typical example of the ineffectiveness of this approach to parental involvement in schools. It is largely a sham because the powers over matters such as curriculum policy are not practically exercised in other than a formal oversight sense. The teachers know more about curriculum development than most parents and they are the ones who are in a position to control these matters. In effect the parents are blissfully unaware of the real curriculum decisions in schools and when they try to intervene, as did some of the Tordale mothers, they are usually outmanoeuvred by teachers.

An essential element of parental participation is time and this appears to present a formidable problem. However, changes to the *gender agenda* of work may provide more flexibility in these respects.

The communication between teachers and parents is vital and this needs to be in more personal forms than the school newsletter. Linfield maintained a regular, lively and informative newsletter, but it was manifestly unable to provide the personal, interactive communication that parents require to be involved in their schools. Through such communication teachers and parents can be more accountable for their teaching and parenting to each other. And it may be possible to broach some of the issues of gender which need to be critiqued if traditional *gender agendas* are to be reconstructed.

In recent years considerable work has been done to challenge the sexism which exists in the classroom (Yates, 1984). Tordale and Linfield probably reflect the effect this has had on most schools. There are limited changes: a few that are part of everyday practice, a few that are pursued by teachers with feminist or egalitarian ideologies, but mostly, the flow of gender differentiated life continues with its various sexist eddies.

If a fair, socially just, society is to be achieved, children need to be prepared for parenting, domestic and breadwinning work—not only by schools, but also through the family and the media. This is not to say that classroom practice cannot or need not be improved. However, the powerful changes are likely to come through changes in the adult world of schooling. Teachers will then work and think differently in their classrooms because of changes made to their own lives. Such teaching will only endure when there is commensurate change to the ways the children's families work, to the messages the media transmit and to the commercial products—especially the horrendously sexist toys—sold for children. However, as schools have a specific task in relation to the construction and reconstruction of social life, it is necessary to address critically the school and school community processes involved in the construction of *gender agendas*.

9 Appendixes

Appendix 9.1 Details of research methods

Quantitative data

One of the first tasks was to collect the precise enrolment details for each school. Each pupil's enrolment card was checked and information about matters such as their age, sex, grade, parents' occupations, numbers of siblings, previous schools attended were recorded. Through the Gippsland Regional Information Bank we obtained 1976 and 1981 census data based on the collection districts which represented the schools' catchment areas. These data included details about marital status, occupations, household incomes, numbers of household occupants, previous places of residence, age, age of leaving school, highest qualification obtained, income etc. In this way we gained a broad social, economic and educational statistical picture of the school communities and could compare this with the information we had collected from the schools.

Document analysis

Some artefacts of social life come in the form of the written doucments which are the lifeblood of our modern bureaucratic society. In schools, especially larger ones, the degree of documentation can be quite substantial. We obtained copies of the 'public' documents which impinged upon or formed part of the operation of the schools. These documents included newsletters to parents, newscuttings about the schools, agendas and minutes of meetings, papers and notices which formed part of the decision making or operation of the schools, memoranda etc. Each of the documents were analysed for their relationship to the research project, and relevant items were used to help structure interviews or to select, analyse and interpret meetings and events.

Observation

Our observation operated at two levels: formal and informal. Informal observation involved the need to maintain a critical awareness and receptiveness to events as they took place during our presence at the schools. Sometimes such observation would develop into informal interviewing as we sought to gain information about the event from the person(s) concerned. In these instances notes were taken as unobtrusively and immediately as possible.

Formal observation of meetings and events occurred where the researchers attended these in their research capacities. In effect such observations were non-participant and note-taking proceeded in an unobtrusive manner throughout. At meetings the observer endeavoured to select a position where all the participants were in view, but with the observer largely out of the immediate line of sight of the participants. This was done to minimise the effect of the observer on the words and actions of the observed.

The data collected in the observations helped to structure the interviews. Frequently, individuals' explanations of events and discussions at meetings etc. were sought in interviews with them. However, the observations provided a continuous, and often interlinked, account of the processes of the formal and informal structures of the schools and of the extent to which gender was a relevant factor therein.

Interviews

The interviews fell into three broad categories:

1) interviews with significant members of the staff, school community and others who had a bearing on important aspects of the schools' operations;
2) interviews with selected teachers in relation to our observation of their classes;
3) interviews with pupils.

All the interviews were organised around mainly open-ended questions from which considerable use was made of follow-up questions. The interviews took place thoughout the project and some people were interviewed several times during the year. One the first occasions when people were interviewed they were asked to recount their biographies from childhood to the present. In particular, we sought their explanations of matters concerning gender in their families, workplaces and schools. In interviews with teachers we specifically sought their views, explanations, expectations and experiences of teaching boys and girls.

The pupils were interviewed in groups of four to minimise any hesitation they had about talking to an interviewer. We selected groups randomly from every grade level in the schools and designed our interview schedules to take account of the ages and intellectual development of the children. We included questions about any differences they saw between boys and girls or men and women, and about the organisation of domestic labour in their homes, their ideas about the sorts of jobs men and women perform and their views about their own future adult roles. Due to the use of group interviews we were often able to record discussion and disagreement between the children on the matters raised.

All interviews were cassette-tape recorded, confidential and transcribed. The pupil interviews were carried out at the end of the project after the classroom observations.

Classroom observations

We selected a class from every grade level in both schools for a week's observation in each. Due to Tordale's size, this meant we observed two of its three classes. However, we also observed the remaining class for a day during trialling of our observation schedule and procedures. One purpose of the classroom observations was to collect quantitative data on the frequencies and durations of interactions which took place between the pupils and their teachers. A recording schedule was developed for the project which enabled the recording of each teacher-pupil interaction, whether it was initiated by the teacher or a male or female pupil, and whether the recipient of each teacher initiated interaction was a male or female pupil. No pupil-pupil or mixed sex group interactions were recorded on the schedule. The type of lesson or activity being performed by the class was also recorded.

The recording of interactions in this way has its limitations in terms of understanding the social processes taking place within a school classroom. However, there are many people, especially policy makers, who place great faith in 'objective' quantifiable evidence. For our purposes it provided a measure of gender differentiation in interactions between teacher and pupils. It also helped to show who initiated any such differentiation.

In addition, we took notes of the qualitative features of the classroom life, including records of particular conversations, comments or instructions. Some of these records formed the basis of interview questions, formal or informal, with the teachers and with some pupil interviews. During the classroom observations close contact was maintained with the teachers throughout the week. Considerable use was made of breaks during the day to informally discuss events with the teachers, and to a lesser extent with the pupils, in order to seek their interpretations and explanations. Notes were made of these discussions as soon as possible afterwards.

Appendix 9.2 Age of Linfield workforce, 1981 (1976)

Age	Males	Females	% Females
15–19	74 (73)	58 (59)	45 (45)
20–24	121 (71)	48 (36)	28 (33)
25–29	89 (86)	26 (26)	23 (23)
30–34	62 (36)	31 (18)	33 (33)
35–39	53 (60)	29 (18)	35 (23)
40–44	72 (60)	33 (45)	31 (43)
45–49	51 (70)	25 (20)	33 (22)
50–54	63 (49)	12 (31)	16 (39)
55–59	34 (37)	11 (9)	24 (20)
60+	23 (28)	6 (6)	21 (18)
Totals	642 (570)	279 (268)	30 (32)

Source: ABS Censuses 1981 (1976)

Appendix 9.3 Age of Tordale workforce, 1981 (1976)

Age	Males	Females	% Females
15–19	4 (9)	3 (7)	43 (44)
20–24	5 (7)	4 (0)	44 (0)
25–29	6 (4)	3 (2)	33 (33)
30–34	7 (4)	3 (2)	30 (33)
35–39	6 (0)	0 (0)	0 (–)
40–44	0 (0)	0 (2)	– (50)
45–49	2 (2)	2 (2)	50 (50)
50–54	5 (6)	3 (0)	38 (0)
55–59	3 (2)	0 (2)	0 (50)
60+	0 (2)	0 (0)	– (0)
Totals	38 (38)	18 (17)	32 (31)

Source: ABS censuses 1981 (1976)

Appendix 9.4 Annual personal income, Linfield, 1976

Amount $	Males	Females	% Females
0– 1499	70	271	80
1500– 6000	167	23	60
6001–12 000	374	66	15
12 001+	50	2	4
Totals	661	592	47

Note: The national male average annual income was approximately $9400.
Source: ABS 1976 Census

Appendix 9.5 Annual personal income, Linfield, 1981

Amount $	Males	Females	% Females
0– 2000	57	258	82
2001– 8000	127	233	65
8001–18 000	450	101	18
18 001+	96	6	6
Totals	730	598	45

Note: The national female and male average annual incomes were approximately $12 000 and $16 000 respectively.
Source: ABS 1981 Census

Appendix 9.6 Annual personal income Tordale, 1976

Amount $	Males	Females	% Females
0– 1499	8	20	71
1500– 6000	24	18	43
6001–12 000	16	0	0
12 001+	0	0	0
Totals	48	38	44

Note: The national male average annual income was approximately $9400.
Source: ABS 1976 Census

Appendix 9.7 Annual personal income, Tordale, 1981

Amount $	Males	Females	% Females
0– 2000	4	17	81
2800– 8000	10	16	62
8001–18 000	26	6	19
18 001+	9	0	0
Totals	49	39	44

Note: The national female and male average annual incomes were approximately $12 000 and $16 000 respectively.
Source: ABS 1981 Census

Appendix 9.8 Occupations of Linfield adults 1981 (1976)

Occupation	Males	Females	% Females
Professional, technical	38 (29)	34 (30)	47 (51)
Administrative	27 (34)	3 (6)	10 (15)
Clerical	24 (17)	68 (68)	74 (80)
Sales	28 (21)	40 (35)	59 (63)
Farmers, etc.	13 (34)	0 (2)	0 (6)
Miners, etc.	3 (3)	0 (0)	0 (0)
Transport, communications	47 (68)	6 (6)	11 (8)
Trades	400 (303)	24 (21)	6 (7)
Services, sports, etc.	25 (30)	56 (56)	69 (65)
Others	17 (12)	21 (28)	55 (70)
Totals	622 (551)	252 (252)	29 (31)

Source: ABS Censuses 1981 (1976)

Appendix 9.9 Occupations of Tordale adults 1981 (1976)

Occupation	Males	Females	% Females
Professional, technical	3 (2)	2 (0)	40 (0)
Administrative	0 (2)	0 (0)	– (0)
Clerical	0 (2)	4 (2)	100 (50)
Sales	2 (4)	7 (6)	78 (60)
Farmers, etc.	2 (8)	0 (4)	0 (33)
Miners, etc.	0 (0)	0 (0)	– (–)
Transport, communications	4 (2)	2 (2)	33 (50)
Trades	26 (16)	2 (0)	7 (0)
Services, sports, etc.	2 (2)	0 (2)	0 (50)
Others	3 (0)	2 (0)	40 (–)
Totals	42 (38)	19 (16)	31 (30)

Source: ABS Censuses 1981 (1976)

Bibliography

Acker, S. (1983) 'Women and Teaching: A Semi-Detached Sociology of a Semi-Profession' in Walker, S. and Barton, L. eds. (1983) *Gender, Class and Education* Lewes: Falmer Press pp. 123–139

Acker, S., Megarry, J., Nisbet, S. and Hoyle, E. eds. (1984) *World Yearbook of Education 1984—Women and Education* London: Kogan Page

Althusser, L. (1971) *Lenin and Philosophy and Other Essays* London: New Left Books

Angus, L. (1985), Human Action and Social Structure in the Study of Schools as Organisations, paper presented to the American Educational Research Association Conference, Chicago, 1985

Angus, L., Prunty, J. and Bates, R. eds. (1984) *Restructuring Victorian Education: Regional Issues* Geelong: Deakin University Press

Apple, M.W. (1971) 'The Hidden Curriculum and the Nature of Conflict' *Interchange* 2, pp. 27–40

—— (1979) *Ideology and Curriculum* London: Routledge and Kegan Paul

—— (1980) 'The Other Side of the Hidden Curriculum: Correspondence Theories and the Labour Process' *Journal of Education* 162, 1, pp. 47–66

—— (1982a) *Education and Power* London: Routledge and Kegan Paul

—— ed. (1982b) *Culture and Economic Reproduction in Education* London: Routledge and Kegan Paul

—— (1983) 'Work, Class and Teaching' in Walker, S. and Barton, L. eds. (1983) *Gender, Class and Education* Lewes: Falmer Press pp. 53–67

Badinter, E. (1981) *The Myth of Motherhood* London: Souvenir Press

Baldock, C. and Cass, B. eds. (1983) *Women, Social Welfare and the State* Sydney: George Allen and Unwin

Bassett, G.W., Jacka, B. and Logan, L. (1982) *The Modern Primary School in Australia* Sydney: George Allen and Unwin

Bates, R. (1984) The Socio-Political Context of Administrative Change, in Angus, L., Prunty, J. and Bates, R. eds. (1984) *Restructuring Victorian Education: Regional Issues* Geelong: Deakin University Press pp. 4–25 reprinted in Frazer, M., Dunstan, J. and Creed, P. eds. (1985) *Perspectives on Organisational Change: Lessons From Education* Melbourne: Longman Cheshire pp. 283–300

Beechey, V. (1979) 'On Patriarchy' *Feminist Review* 3, pp. 66–82

Bell, C. and Encel, S. eds. (1978) *Inside the Whale* Sydney: Pergamon
Berger, P. and Luckmann, T. (1967) *The Social Construction of Reality* Harmondsworth: Penguin
Bessant, B and Spaull, A. (1972) *Teachers in Conflict* Melbourne: Melbourne University Press
Blackburn Report, Vols. 1 and 2 (1985) Melbourne: The Ministerial Review of Postcompulsory Schooling
Bourdieu, P. (1977) *Outline of a Theory of Practice* Cambridge: Cambridge University Press
Bourdieu, P. and Passeron, J.C. (1977) *Reproduction in Education, Society and Culture* London: Sage
Bowlby, J.A. (1953) *Childcare and the Growth of Love* Harmondsworth: Pelican
—— (1971) *Attachment and Loss* Harmondsworth: Penguin
Brophy, J.E. and Good, T.L. (1974) *Teacher-Student Relationships* New York: Holt, Rinehart and Winston
Bryson, L. (1984) The Australian Patriarchal Family, in Encel, S. and Bryson, L. eds. (1984) *Australian Society* 4th edn, Melbourne: Longman Cheshire, pp. 113–169
Burns, A., Bottomley, G. and Jools, P. eds. (1983) *The Family in the Modern World* Sydney: George Allen and Unwin
Byrne, E.M. (1978) *Women and Education* London: Tavistock
Clarricoates, K. (1978) 'Dinosaurs in the Classroom: a Re-examination of Some Aspects of the "Hidden" Curriculum in Primary Schools' *Women's Studies International Quarterly* 1, 4, pp. 353–364
—— (1980) The Importance of Being Ernest...Emma...Tom...Jane, in Deem, R. ed. (1980) *Schooling for Women's Work* London: Routledge and Kegan Paul, pp. 26–41
Coats, M. (1983) Gender, Class and Education: a Teaching Bibliography of European Studies, in Walker, S. and Barton, L. eds. (1983) *Gender, Class and Education* Lewes: Falmer Press pp. 173–182
Commonwealth Education Commissions (1983) *Participation and Equity: Funding Guidelines to the Commonwealth Education Commissions* Canberra: Australian Government Publishing Service
Commonwealth Schools Commission, (1975) *Girls, School and Society* Canberra: Commonwealth Schools Commission
—— (1983) *Participation and Equality in Australian Schools: the Goal of Full Secondary Education* Canberra: Australian Government Publishing Service
—— (1984) *Girls and Tomorrow* Canberra: Commonwealth School Commission
Connell, R.W. (1983) *Which Way Is Up?* Sydney: George Allen and Unwin
—— (1984) *Teachers' Work* Sydney: George Allen and Unwin
Connell, R.W., Ashenden, D.J., Kessler, S. and Dowsett, G.W. (1982) *Making the Difference* Sydney: George Allen and Unwin
Corbett, J. (1987) 'Parents: why leave' *Ms Muffett* 32, June: 28–9
Cosgrove, S. (1981) 'Do You Discriminate Against Girls in Your Classroom?' *South Australian Secondary Teachers' Association Journal* December, No. 813

David, M.E. (1982) *The State, The Family and Education* London: Routledge and Kegan Paul
Davies, L. (1984) *Pupil Power: Deviance and Gender in School* Lewes: Falmer Press
Deem, R. (1978) *Women and Schooling* London: Routledge and Kegan Paul
—— ed. (1980) *Schooling for Women's Work* London: Routledge and Kegan Paul
Delamont, S. (1976) *Interaction in the Classroom* London: Methuen
—— (1980a) *Sex Roles and the School* London: Methuen
—— (1980b) *The Sociology of Women* London: George Allen and Unwin
Dunlop, F. (1982) 'The Ideas of Male and Female' *Journal of Philosophy of Education* 16,2, pp. 209–222
Edgar, D.E. (1980) *An Introduction to Australian Society* Sydney: Prentice-Hall
Education Department of Victoria, Policy and Planning Unit (1984) *Women in the Education Department of Victoria* Melbourne: Education Department of Victoria
Education Victoria (1986) vol.1, no.1., February
Elliott, J. (1974) Sex Role Constraints on Freedom of Discussion, *The New Era* 55, 6, pp. 147–155
Engels, F. (1968) The Origin of the Family, Private Property and the State, in Marx, K. and Engels, F. 1968 *Selected Works Volume One* London: Lawrence and Wisehart
Evans, T.D. (1979) 'Creativity, Sex-Role Socialisation and Pupil-Teacher Interactions in Early Schooling' *Sociological Review* 27, 1, pp. 139–155
—— (1980) 'Pre-School and Primary School Teachers' Interaction With Their Most and Least Creative Pupils' *Research in Education,* 24: 31–43
—— (1982a) 'Being and Becoming: Teachers' Perceptions of Sex-Roles and Actions Toward Their Male and Female Pupils' *British Journal of Sociology of Education* 3, 2, pp. 127–143
—— (1982b) *Girls and Jobs: Improving the Odds* Churchill: Gippsland Institute of Advanced Education
—— (1983) Gender, Class and Education: a Teaching Bibliography of Australian and New Zealand Studies, in Walker, S. and Barton, L. eds. (1983) *Gender, Class and Education* Lewes: Falmer Press pp. 183–189
—— (1984a) *Community School* Churchill: Gippsland Institute of Advanced Education
—— (1984b) *Changing School* Churchill: Gippsland Institute of Advanced Education
—— (1984c) Gender Differentiation and Interaction in Australian Primary Schools, in Acker, S. et al. eds. (1984) *World Yearbook of Education—Women and Education* London: Kogan Page pp. 90–99
—— (1987) 'Gender and Primary Schooling in Australia: Some Classroom and Curriculum Findings' *Journal of Curriculum Studies* 19, 2 pp. 183–6
—— (1987) 'Gender and Primary Schooling in Australia: Shaping Policies and Making Decisions' *Journal of Curriculum Studies* 19, 3 pp. 271–3
—— Evans, T.D. and Nation, D.E. (1984) Families, Schooling and Work in the Latrobe Valley, *Proceedings of the Australian Family Research*

Conference 1983 Volume Four Melbourne: Institute of Family Studies pp. 227–263
Firkin, J. (1983) The Education of Women and Girls, Has Fantasy Ran Away With Reality? Australian College of Education, New South Wales Chapter 24th Annual Conference May, 1983
Flanders, N. (1970) *Analyzing Teacher Behaviour* New York: Addison-Wesley
Foggo, D. (1985) 'Women in Teacher Unions' *Ms Muffet* 26, pp. 18–19
—— (1986) 'The Scene is Set for Change' *Australian Teacher* 15, pp. 4–6
Frameworks (1985) Melbourne: Education Department of Victoria
Frazer, M., Dunstan, J. and Creed, P. eds. 1985 *Perspectives on Organisational Change: Lessons From Education* Melbourne: Longman Cheshire
Fuller, M. (1979) Dimensions of Gender in a School, PhD thesis, University of Bristol, cited in Davies, L. (1984)
—— (1980) Black Girls in a London Comprehensive School in Deem, R. ed. (1980) *Schooling For Women's* Work London: Routledge and Kegan Paul pp. 52–65
Gaskell, J. (1983) 'The Reproduction of Family Life' *British Journal of Sociology of Education* 4, 1, pp. 19–38
Giddens, A. 1979 *Central Problems in Social Theory* London: Macmillan
—— (1981) *The Class Structure of Advanced Societies* London: Hutchinson
—— (1984) *The Constitution of Society* London: Polity Press
Giroux, H.A. (1983) 'Theories of Reproduction and Resistance in the New Sociology of Education' *Harvard Educational Review* 53, 3, pp. 257–293
Giroux, H.A. and Purpel, D. eds. (1983) *The Hidden Curriculum and Moral Education* Berkeley: McCutchan
Hargreaves, D.H. (1967) *Social Relations in a Secondary School* London: Routledge and Kegan Paul
Hargreaves, D.H., Hester S.K. and Mellor (1975) *Deviance in Classrooms* London: Routledge and Kegan Paul
Hunt, A.J. (1985) A Government Thrust Towards Change in Frazer, M., Dunstan, J. and Creed, P. eds. (1985) *Perspectives on Organisational Change: Lessons From Education* Melbourne: Longman Cheshire pp. 13–32
Jackson, P.W. (1968) *Life in Classrooms* New York: Holt, Rinehart and Winston
Lacey, C. (1970) *Hightown Grammar* Manchester: Manchester University Press
—— (1977) *The Socialisation of Teachers* London: Methuen
Leder, G. (1986) Teacher-Student Interactions—A Hidden Message, paper presented at the Australian Association for Research in Education Conference, Melbourne, November, 1986
Levy, B. (1974) Do School Sell Girls Short? in Stacey et al eds. (1974) *And Jill Came Tumbling After* New York: Dell
Lewin, E. and Olesen, V. (1981) 'Lateralness in Women's Work: New Views on Success' *Sex Roles* 6, pp. 619–630
Llewellyn, M. (1980) Studying Girls at School: the Implications of Confusion in Deem, R. ed. (1980) pp. 42–51
Lortie, D.C. (1975) *School Teacher* Chicago: Chicago University Press

Matthews, J.J. (1984) *Good and Mad Women* Sydney: George Allen and Unwin

McRobbie, A. and McCabe, T. eds. (1981) *Feminism for Girls* London: Routledge and Kegan Paul

Meisner, M. (1975) 'No Exit for Wives: Sexual Division of Labour and the Cumulation of Household Demands' *Canadian Review of Sociology and Anthropology* 12, pp. 424–439

Ministerial Paper No. 4, School Councils (1983) Melbourne: Education Department of Victoria

Mitchell, J. (1971) *Woman's Estate* Harmondsworth: Penguin

—— (1974) *Psychoanalysis and Feminism* London: Allen Lane

Morgan, D.H.J. (1981) Men, Masculinity and the Process of Sociological Inquiry in Roberts, H. ed. (1981) *Doing Feminist Research* London: Routledge and Kegan Paul pp. 83–113

Moskowitz, E.J. (1983) Gender, Class and Education: a Teaching Bibliography of American Studies, in Walker, S. and Barton, L. (1983) pp. 191–213

Nation, D.E. (1983) *Girls and Jobs* (Video) Churchill: Gippsland Institute of Advanced Education

Oakley, A. (1974a) *Housewife* London: Allen Lane

—— (1974b) *The Sociology of Housework* Oxford: Martin Robertson

—— (1981) Interviewing women a contradiction in terms in Roberts, H. ed. (1981) *Doing Feminist Research* London: Routledge and Kegan Paul pp. 30–61

—— (1984) *Taking It Like A Woman* London: Jonathon Cape

Ochiltree, G. and Amato, P. (1985) *The Child's Eye View of Family Life* Melbourne: Institute of Family Studies

Ollerenshaw, K. and Flude, C. (1974) *Returning to Teaching* Lancaster: University Press

Palardy, J. (1969) 'What Teachers Believe—What Teachers Achieve' *Elementary School Journal* 69 pp. 370–374

Ramsay, E. (1984) 'Language, Politics and Sexism in the Classroom' *Education News* 18, 3 pp. 20–23

Report of the Ministerial Review of Educational Services for the Disabled (1984) Melbourne: Government Printer

Rubin, G. (1975) The Traffic in Women: Notes on the 'Political Economy' of Sex, in Reiter, R.R. ed. (1975) *Towards an Anthropology of Women* New York: Monthly Review Press

Russell, G. (1979) 'Fathers! Incompetent or Reluctant Parents?' *Australian and New Zealand Journal of Sociology* 15, 1, pp. 57–65

—— (1983) *The Changing Role of Fathers* St Lucia: University of Queensland Press

Sampson, (1975) *The Australian Women's Weekly* and the Aspirations of Girls, in Edgar, D.E. ed. (1975) *The Sociology of Australian Education* Sydney: McGraw-Hill, pp. 248–257

—— (1983) The Role of Women in Leadership in Australian Schools, in Browne, R. and Foster, L. eds. (1983) *Sociology of Education* Melbourne: Macmillan, pp. 417–423

—— (1986a) Teacher Careers and Promotion in Australia, in Schmuck, P.

ed. (1986) *Women as Educators* New York: University of New York Press, pp. 47–64
—— (1986b) Teachers are Traditional Role Models, paper presented to the Australian Association for Research in Education Conference, Melbourne, November, 1986
Spaull, A. and Hince, K. (1986) *Industrial Relations and State Education in Australia* Melbourne: A.E. Press
Spender, D. (1980) Talking in Class, in Spender, D. and Sarah, E. eds. (1980) *Learning to Lose* London: Women's Press pp. 148–154
—— (1982) *Invisible Women* London: Writers and Readers
Spender, D. and Sarah, E. eds. (1980) *Learning to Lose* London: Women's Press
Stanworth, M. (1981) *Gender and Schooling* London: Women's Research and Resources Centre
Steward, S. and Garratt, S. (1984) *Signed, Sealed and Delivered* London: Pluto Press
Summers, A. (1975) *Damned Whores and God's Police* Melbourne: Penguin
Taylor, S. (1980) 'School Experience and Student Experience and Student Perspectives: A Study of Some Effects of Secondary School Organisation' *Educational Review* 31, 1
—— (1982) 'Schooling and Social Reproduction' *Australian Jornal of Education* 26, 2, pp. 144–154
Technological Change in Australia (1980) Report of the Committee of Inquiry into Technological Change in Australia, Canberra: Australian Government Publishing Service
Tolson, A. (1977) *The Limits of Masculinity* London: Tavistock
Victorian Committee on Equal Opportunity in Schools (1977) *Report to the Premier of Victoria* Melbourne: Government Printer
Wajcman, J. and Rosewarne, S. (1986) 'The "Feminisation" of Work', *Australian Society* 5, 9: 15–17
Wearing, B. (1984) *The Ideology of Motherhood* Sydney: George Allen and Unwin
Wentworth, R. (1979) 'A Comparison of the Career Aspirations of Men and Women Trainee Teachers' *South Pacific Journal of Teacher Education* 7, 3 and 4 pp. 85–91
Wild, R. (1985) 'Some Problems of Contract Research in Sociology' *Australian and New Zealand Journal of Sociology* 21, 2, pp. 258–266
Williams, C. (1981) *Open Cut* Sydney: George Allen and Unwin
Willis, P. (1977) *Learning to Labour* Farnborough: Saxon House
Woods, P. ed. (1980) *Pupil Strategies* London: Croom Helm
Yates, L. (1984) Counter Sexist Strategies in Australian Schools, in Acker, S. et al. eds. (1984) *World Yearbook of Education—Women and Education* London: Kogan Page pp. 279–281
—— (1985) 'Curriculum Becomes our Way of Contradicting Biology and Culture–An Outline of Some Dilemmas for Non-Sexist Education' *Australian Journal of Education* 29, 1, pp. 3–16
—— (1987) Australian Research on Gender and Education 1975–1985, in Keeves, J. ed. (1987) *Australian Education: review of recent research* Sydney: Allen and Unwin, pp. 241–268

Index

A Gender Agenda

Studies in Society

Titles include:

The Migrant Presence Martin
Social Stratification in Australia Wild
Race Class and Rebellion in the South Pacific Mamak and Ali
Children and Families in Australia Burns and Goodnow
Johnsonville Pearson
Australian Community Studies and Beyond Wild
Open Cut Williams
The Ethnic Dimension Martin/Encel
The Aging Experience Russell
Australian Cinema Tulloch
Strikes in Australia Waters
Class Consciousness in Australia Chamberlain
Heathcote Wild
Practice and Belief Black/Glasner
Law, Capitalism and Democrary O'Malley
Eclipse of Equality Pearson and Thorns
The Family in the Modern World Burns, Jools and Bottomley
Medical Dominance Willis
Women, Social Welfare and the State Baldock/Cass
Ideology of Motherhood Wearing
Indians in a White Australia de Lepervanche
Confronting School and Work Dwyer, Wilson and Woock
Ethnicity, Class and Gender in Australia Bottomley/de Lepervanche
The Faith of Australians Mol
Social Theory and the Australian City Kilmartin/Thorns/Burke
The First Wave Lewins/Ly
Surveys in Social Research de Vaus
Australian Ways Manderson
Custody and Control Asher
Where it Hurts Russell and Schofield
Yellow Cake and Crocodiles Lea and Zehner
Caring for Australia's Children Brennan and O'Donnell
Shaping Futures Wilson and Wyn